The primer set furth by the Kinges maiestie [and] his clergie, to be taught, lerned, and red, and none other to be vsed thorowout his highnes dominions. (1547)

Church of England

The primer set furth by the Kinges maiestie [and] his clergie, to be taught, lerned, and red, and none other to be vsed thorowout his highnes dominions.

Book of hours.
Church of England.
Imprint from colophon.
At foot of title: Cum priuilegio ad imprimendum solum.
Signatures: a4 (-a4) A-U4 2A-2G4 2H2 .
Printed in red and black.
The last leaf has printer's device (McKerrow 104) on verso.
In this edition, title has: his highnes dominions.
[226] p.
[Imprinted at London : The last daie of Nouember, in the first yere of the reigne of our souereigne lord kyng Edvvard the. VI. By Rychard Grafton. printer to his moste royall Maiestie, In the yere of our Lord M.D.X.LVII [1547]]
STC (2nd ed.) / 16048a
English
Reproduction of the original in the Bodleian Library

Early English Books Online (EEBO) Editions

Imagine holding history in your hands.

Now you can. Digitally preserved and previously accessible only through libraries as Early English Books Online, this rare material is now available in single print editions. Thousands of books written between 1475 and 1700 and ranging from religion to astronomy, medicine to music, can be delivered to your doorstep in individual volumes of high-quality historical reproductions.

We have been compiling these historic treasures for more than 70 years. Long before such a thing as "digital" even existed, ProQuest founder Eugene Power began the noble task of preserving the British Museum's collection on microfilm. He then sought out other rare and endangered titles, providing unparalleled access to these works and collaborating with the world's top academic institutions to make them widely available for the first time. This project furthers that original vision.

These texts have now made the full journey -- from their original printing-press versions available only in rare-book rooms to online library access to new single volumes made possible by the partnership between artifact preservation and modern printing technology. A portion of the proceeds from every book sold supports the libraries and institutions that made this collection possible, and that still work to preserve these invaluable treasures passed down through time.

This is history, traveling through time since the dawn of printing to your own personal library.

Initial Proquest EEBO Print Editions collections include:

Early Literature

This comprehensive collection begins with the famous Elizabethan Era that saw such literary giants as Chaucer, Shakespeare and Marlowe, as well as the introduction of the sonnet. Traveling through Jacobean and Restoration literature, the highlight of this series is the Pollard and Redgrave 1475-1640 selection of the rarest works from the English Renaissance.

Early Documents of World History

This collection combines early English perspectives on world history with documentation of Parliament records, royal decrees and military documents that reveal the delicate balance of Church and State in early English government. For social historians, almanacs and calendars offer insight into daily life of common citizens. This exhaustively complete series presents a thorough picture of history through the English Civil War.

Historical Almanacs

Historically, almanacs served a variety of purposes from the more practical, such as planting and harvesting crops and plotting nautical routes, to predicting the future through the movements of the stars. This collection provides a wide range of consecutive years of "almanacks" and calendars that depict a vast array of everyday life as it was several hundred years ago.

Early History of Astronomy & Space

Humankind has studied the skies for centuries, seeking to find our place in the universe. Some of the most important discoveries in the field of astronomy were made in these texts recorded by ancient stargazers, but almost as impactful were the perspectives of those who considered their discoveries to be heresy. Any independent astronomer will find this an invaluable collection of titles arguing the truth of the cosmic system.

Early History of Industry & Science

Acting as a kind of historical Wall Street, this collection of industry manuals and records explores the thriving industries of construction; textile, especially wool and linen; salt; livestock; and many more.

Early English Wit, Poetry & Satire

The power of literary device was never more in its prime than during this period of history, where a wide array of political and religious satire mocked the status quo and poetry called humankind to transcend the rigors of daily life through love, God or principle. This series comments on historical patterns of the human condition that are still visible today.

Early English Drama & Theatre

This collection needs no introduction, combining the works of some of the greatest canonical writers of all time, including many plays composed for royalty such as Queen Elizabeth I and King Edward VI. In addition, this series includes history and criticism of drama, as well as examinations of technique.

Early History of Travel & Geography

Offering a fascinating view into the perception of the world during the sixteenth and seventeenth centuries, this collection includes accounts of Columbus's discovery of the Americas and encompasses most of the Age of Discovery, during which Europeans and their descendants intensively explored and mapped the world. This series is a wealth of information from some the most groundbreaking explorers.

Early Fables & Fairy Tales

This series includes many translations, some illustrated, of some of the most well-known mythologies of today, including Aesop's Fables and English fairy tales, as well as many Greek, Latin and even Oriental parables and criticism and interpretation on the subject.

Early Documents of Language & Linguistics

The evolution of English and foreign languages is documented in these original texts studying and recording early philology from the study of a variety of languages including Greek, Latin and Chinese, as well as multilingual volumes, to current slang and obscure words. Translations from Latin, Hebrew and Aramaic, grammar treatises and even dictionaries and guides to translation make this collection rich in cultures from around the world.

Early History of the Law

With extensive collections of land tenure and business law "forms" in Great Britain, this is a comprehensive resource for all kinds of early English legal precedents from feudal to constitutional law, Jewish and Jesuit law, laws about public finance to food supply and forestry, and even "immoral conditions." An abundance of law dictionaries, philosophy and history and criticism completes this series.

Early History of Kings, Queens and Royalty

This collection includes debates on the divine right of kings, royal statutes and proclamations, and political ballads and songs as related to a number of English kings and queens, with notable concentrations on foreign rulers King Louis IX and King Louis XIV of France, and King Philip II of Spain. Writings on ancient rulers and royal tradition focus on Scottish and Roman kings, Cleopatra and the Biblical kings Nebuchadnezzar and Solomon.

Early History of Love, Marriage & Sex

Human relationships intrigued and baffled thinkers and writers well before the postmodern age of psychology and self-help. Now readers can access the insights and intricacies of Anglo-Saxon interactions in sex and love, marriage and politics, and the truth that lies somewhere in between action and thought.

Early History of Medicine, Health & Disease

This series includes fascinating studies on the human brain from as early as the 16th century, as well as early studies on the physiological effects of tobacco use. Anatomy texts, medical treatises and wound treatment are also discussed, revealing the exponential development of medical theory and practice over more than two hundred years.

Early History of Logic, Science and Math

The "hard sciences" developed exponentially during the 16th and 17th centuries, both relying upon centuries of tradition and adding to the foundation of modern application, as is evidenced by this extensive collection. This is a rich collection of practical mathematics as applied to business, carpentry and geography as well as explorations of mathematical instruments and arithmetic; logic and logicians such as Aristotle and Socrates; and a number of scientific disciplines from natural history to physics.

Early History of Military, War and Weaponry

Any professional or amateur student of war will thrill at the untold riches in this collection of war theory and practice in the early Western World. The Age of Discovery and Enlightenment was also a time of great political and religious unrest, revealed in accounts of conflicts such as the Wars of the Roses.

Early History of Food

This collection combines the commercial aspects of food handling, preservation and supply to the more specific aspects of canning and preserving, meat carving, brewing beer and even candy-making with fruits and flowers, with a large resource of cookery and recipe books. Not to be forgotten is a "the great eater of Kent," a study in food habits.

Early History of Religion

From the beginning of recorded history we have looked to the heavens for inspiration and guidance. In these early religious documents, sermons, and pamphlets, we see the spiritual impact on the lives of both royalty and the commoner. We also get insights into a clergy that was growing ever more powerful as a political force. This is one of the world's largest collections of religious works of this type, revealing much about our interpretation of the modern church and spirituality.

Early Social Customs

Social customs, human interaction and leisure are the driving force of any culture. These unique and quirky works give us a glimpse of interesting aspects of day-to-day life as it existed in an earlier time. With books on games, sports, traditions, festivals, and hobbies it is one of the most fascinating collections in the series.

old books. new life.

The BiblioLife Network

This project was made possible in part by the BiblioLife Network (BLN), a project aimed at addressing some of the huge challenges facing book preservationists around the world. The BLN includes libraries, library networks, archives, subject matter experts, online communities and library service providers. We believe every book ever published should be available as a high-quality print reproduction; printed on-demand anywhere in the world. This insures the ongoing accessibility of the content and helps generate sustainable revenue for the libraries and organizations that work to preserve these important materials.

The following book is in the "public domain" and represents an authentic reproduction of the text as printed by the original publisher. While we have attempted to accurately maintain the integrity of the original work, there are sometimes problems with the original work or the micro-film from which the books were digitized. This can result in minor errors in reproduction. Possible imperfections include missing and blurred pages, poor pictures, markings and other reproduction issues beyond our control. Because this work is culturally important, we have made it available as part of our commitment to protecting, preserving, and promoting the world's literature.

GUIDE TO FOLD-OUTS MAPS and OVERSIZED IMAGES

The book you are reading was digitized from microfilm captured over the past thirty to forty years. Years after the creation of the original microfilm, the book was converted to digital files and made available in an online database.

In an online database, page images do not need to conform to the size restrictions found in a printed book. When converting these images back into a printed bound book, the page sizes are standardized in ways that maintain the detail of the original. For large images, such as fold-out maps, the original page image is split into two or more pages

Guidelines used to determine how to split the page image follows:

• Some images are split vertically; large images require vertical and horizontal splits.
• For horizontal splits, the content is split left to right.
• For vertical splits, the content is split from top to bottom.
• For both vertical and horizontal splits, the image is processed from top left to bottom right.

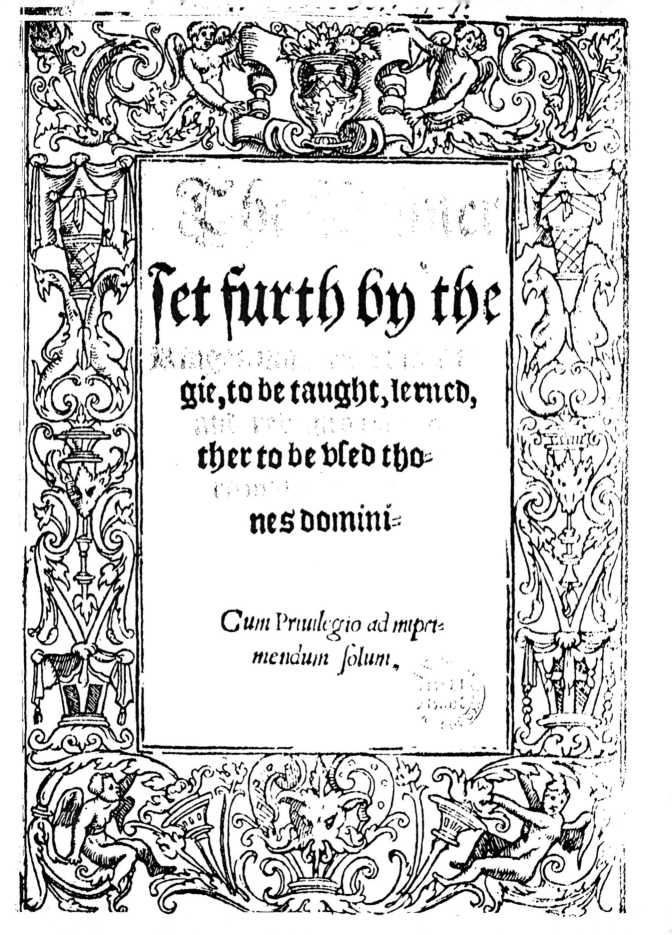

set furth by the

gie, to be taught, lerned,

ther to be vsed tho=

nes domini=

Cum Priuilegio ad impri-
mendum solum.

An Almanacke for .xv. yeres.

	The Sondaies letter.	The golden nombre.	The dayes of the monethes.	The lepe yere.
M.d.xlvii.	B	ix	x.April.	C
M.d.xlviii.	A	x	i.April.	
M.d.xlix.	F	xi	xxi.April.	
M.d.l.	E	xii	vi.April.	
M.d.li.	D	xiii	xxix.Marche	
M.d.lii.	C	xiiii	xvii.April.	X
M.d.liii.	A	xv	ii.April.	
M.d.liiii.	G	xvi	xxv.Marche.	
M.d.lv.	F	xvii	xiiii.April.	
M.d.lvi.	E	xviii	v.April.	H
M.d.lvii.	L	xix	xviii.April.	
M.d.lviii.	B	i	x.April.	
M.d.lix.	A	ii	xxvi.Marche.	
M.d.lx.	B	iii	xiiii.April.	J
M.d.lxi.	E	iiii	vi.April.	

The Kalender.

January hath.xxxj. February hath.xxviii

	d
	e f
xix	g
viii	
	b
xvi	c d e
v	
xiii	f g
ii	
	b c
x	
xviii	d e
vii	
	f g
xv	
iiii	b c d e
xvii	
vi	f g
ix	b c
	d e
xvii	f g
vi	
	b
xiiii	c

Sol in Pic.

a.ij

KL Marche hath. xxx. dayes.   KL April hath. xxx. dayes.

iii	d	xi	b
xi	e		c
	f	xix	d
xix	g	viii	e
viii	a	xvi	f
	b	v	g
xvi	c		a
v	d	xiii	b
	e	ii	c
xiii	f		d
ii	g	**Sol in Tau.**	e
Sol in Aries.	a		f
	b	xviii	g
	c	vii	a
	d	**Kalen. May**	b
	e		c
xviii	f		d
vii	g	xv	e
Kalen. Aprilis	a	xiii	f
	b		g
	c		a
xv	d		b
xiii	e	xii	c
	f	i	d
xii	g	ix	e
i	a		f
	b		g
Annunciation of our Lady.	c	xvii	a
	d	vi	b
xvii	e		c
vi	f	xiiii	d
	g	iii	e
xiiii	a		f
iii			g

KL Maye hath. xxxi. dayes.   KL June hath. xxx. dayes.

	Maye		June
xi	Philip and Jacob Apost	xvi v	
xix viii		viii xvi v	
xvi v		xiii ii	
xiii ii			
x		p	
xviii vii		xviii vii	S. Barnabe
xv iiii	Kalen. June.	xv iiii	Kalen. July
xii i	Sol in Gemi.	xii	Sol in Cancro.
ix		p	
xvii vi		xvii vi	
xiiii iii		xiiii iii	Nativite of Saint Iohn.
xi xix viii		xi xix	Peter and Paule Apost.

KL July hath xxxi.dayes.   KL August hath xxx.dayes.

xix	g			viii	c	
viii				xvi	d	
	b			v	e	
xvi	c				f	
v	d			xiii	g	
	e			ii	a	
xiii	f				b	
ii	g			x	c	
	a			xviii	d	
	b			vii	e	
xviii	c				f	
vii	d			xv	g	
	e			iiii	a	
xv	f	Sol in Leo.			b	
iiii	g				c	
	a				d	Sol in Virgo.
xii	b			xii	e	
i	c			i	f	
	d				g	
ix	e	Mary mag	Mag	ix	a	
	f			xvii	b	S. Bartho.
xvii	g	James Apoſt.		vi	c	
vi	a				d	
	b			xiiii	e	
xiiii	c			iii	f	
iii	d				g	
	e			xi	a	
xi	f				b	
	g				c	
xix	a				d	

Ur father whiche art in heauen
halowed be thy name.

Thy kyngdome come.

Thy will be done in yearthe
as it is in heauen.

Geue vs this daie our dayly
bread.

And forgeue vs our trespasses as we forgeue
theim that trespace against vs.

And let vs not be lead into temptacion.

But deliuer vs from euill. Amen.

¶ The salutacion of the auugell to the
blessed virgin Mary.

Aile Mary full of grace, the Lorde is with
the: Blessed art thou among women & bles=
sed is the fruite of th, wombe. Amen.

¶ The Crede or. xii. articles of the christen faith.

Beleue in GOD the father almightie
maker of heauen and yearth.

And in Jesu Christ his onely sonne
our Lorde.

Which was conceiued by the holy Ghost, borne
of the virgin Mary.

Suffered vnder ponce Pilate, was crucified
dedde, buried, and descended into hell.

And the third daie, he arose agayne from death.

He ascended to heauen, and sitteth on the right
hande of God the father almightie.

From thence he shall come to iudge the quicke
and the dedde.

I beleue in the holy ghost.

J. L.   The

The holy catholique Churche.

The communion of sainctes : The forgeuenes of synnes.

The resurreccion of the body.

And the life euerlasting. Amen.

The .x. commaundementes of almightie God.

Thou shalt haue none other Goddes but me.

Thou shalt not haue any grauen Image nor any likenesse of any thig y in is heaue aboue, or in earth, beneth, or in the water vnderthe yearth, to the intent to do any godly honor or worship vnto them.

Thou shalt not take the name of thy Lord God in vaine.

Remembre that thou kepe holy the sabboth day.

Honour thy father and thy mother.

Thou shalt do no mordre.

Thou shalt not commit adultery.

Thou shalt not steale.

Thou shalt not beare false wittnesse agaynst thy neighbour.

Thou shalt not vniustly desire thy neighbours house, nor thy neighbours wife, nor his seruaunt, nor his maide, nor his Oxe, nor his Asse, nor any thyng that is thy neighbours.

Lord, into thy handes I commend my spirite.

Thou hast redemed me, Lord God of truth.

Grace before dynner.

The iyes of all thynges trust in the, O Lorde thou geuest them meate in due season. Thou
doest

doest open thy hand, and fillest with thy blessyng
every liuyng thyng. Good lord blesse vs & thy gyf=
tes whiche we receiue of thy bounteous liberali=
tie: Through Christ our lorde. Amen.

The kyng of eternall glory, make vs parteners
of the heauenly table. Amen.

God is charitie, and he that dwelleth in chari=
tie dwelleth in God, and God in hym: God graunt
vs all to dwell in hym. Amen.

Grace after dynner.

THe God of peace and loue, vouchesafe alwaie
to dwell with vs: And thou Lord haue mer=
cie vpon vs.

Glory, honor, and prayse be vnto the O GOD
whiche hast fed vs from our tender age, and ge=
uest sustinaunce to euery lyuyng thyng: Replenish
oure hartes with ioye and gladnesse, that we al=
waie hauyng sufficient, maie be riche and plenti=
full in all goodwoorkes, through our Lord Iesu
Christ. Amen.

Lorde haue mercy vpon vs.
Christ haue mercy vpon vs.
Lorde haue mercy vpon vs.
Our father whiche art in heauen. &c.
Let vs not be led into temptacion,
But deliuer vs from euill.
Lorde heare my praier,
And let my crie come to the.

From y fierie dartes of the deuil, bothe in weale
and wo, our sauiour Christ be our defence bucke=
ler and sheilde. Amen.

A. ij.   God

God saue the Churche, our Kyng and realme,
and God haue mercie vpon all Christian soules,
Amen.

Grace before supper.

O Lord Jesu Christ, without whom nothyng
is swete nor sauery, we besech thee to blesse
vs and our supper, and with thy blessed presence
to chere and happee, that in all our meates and
drynkes, we maie taste and sauor of thee to thy
honor and glory. amen.

Grace after supper.

Blessed is God in all his giftes: and holy in
all his workes.

Our helpe is in the name of the lord: who hath
made bothe heauen and yearth.

Blessed be the name of our lorde: from hence,
furthe world without ende.

Moste mightie lorde and mercifull father,
we yeld thee hartie thankes for our bodely
sustenaunce: requirynge also moste entierly thy
gracious goodnes, so to feede vs with the foode
of thy heauenly grace that wee maie worthely glorifie thy holy name in this
life, and after bee partakers of
the lyfe euerlastynge:
through our lorde
Jesus Christ.
Amen.
God saue the Church, our Kyng, and
realme, and God haue mercie on
al Christian soules. amen.

 **LORD** open thou my lippes.

And my mouthe, shall shewe thy praise.

O God, to helpe me make good spede.

Lorde, make haste to succour me.

Glory be to the father, & to the sonne and to the holy ghost.

As it was in the beginning, and is now, and euer shalbe, worlde with=out ende. Amen.

Venite exultemus, Psal. xciiii.

A song stirring to the prayse of God.

Ome and let vs reioyce vnto the Lorde, let vs ioyfully syng to God our sauiour, let vs come before his face with confession and thankesgeuing, and syng we ioyfully vnto hym in Psalmes.

A. iii.   Fo

For God is a great lord, and a great kyng ouer all godes, whiche doth not forsake his people, in whose power are all the costes of the yearth, & he beholdeth the toppes of the mountaines.

The sea is his, for he hath made it, & his handes haue fashioned the yearth also: come therfore and let vs worshyp and fal doune before God, let vs wepe before the Lorde, who hath made vs, for he is our Lorde God, & wee are his people and the shepe of his pasture.

To daie if ye here his voice se that ye harde not your hartes as in the bitter murmuring in the tyme of temptacion in wildernes, wher your fathers tēpted me, proued me, & sawe my workes.

Fortie yeres was I greued with this generacion, and I saied euer they erre in their hartes, they haue not knowen my wayes, to whome I swore in myne angre, that they shoulde not entre into my rest.

Hayle Mary full of grace, the. &c.

Glory be to the. &c. As it was in. &c.

The

The himpne.   I am lucis orto, &c,

NOw the cherefull daye dooth spryng:
Unto god pray we and singe:
That in all workes of the day,
He preserue and kepe vs aye.
    That our toungue we may refrain.
From all strief and wordes vayne.
Kepe our iyes in couerture,
From all euill and vayne pleasure.
    That our hartes bee voyded quite.
From phansy and fonde delight.
Thinne diet of drincke and meate
Of the fleshe to coole the heate.
    That whē the day hence doth wēd,
And the course the nighte doeth send,
By forbering thinges wordely,
Our God we maye glorifie. Amen.

Domine dominus noster Psal.viii.
    Of the praise, and honor
and glory of Christ

Lorde, whiche art our Lord.
how meruailous is thy name
ouer all the yearth:
    For thy magnificence, is exalted a-
boue the heauens.

                       Thou

Thou hast auaunced thy prayse, by the mouthes of infantes, a suckyng babes in dispite of thyne enemies, for to confound the aduersary and reuenger

For I shall behold the heauens, whiche are the worke of thy fingers, the Moone and the Sterres, whyche thou hast ordeined.

What is man that thou art so mindfull of hym? Or what is the sonne of man that thou so regardest hym?

Thou hast made hym somwhat inferior to aungels, thou haste crouned him with glory and honour, and haste made hym Lorde vpon the workes of thyne handes.

Thou hast put all thynges in subiection vnder his feete: All maner of shepe and oxen, yea, moreouer the cattell of the fielde, fowles of the aire, and fishes of the sea, whiche walke in the pathes of the sea.

O Lorde which art our Lord, how maruellous is thy name ouer all the yearth?

Glory

Glory be to the father, and to the.&c.
As it was in the beginnyng, and is
now, and euer shalbe.&c.Amen.

Cœli enarrant, Psal.xviii

Of the glorie of God, whiche is shewed
by hys creatures, and of his holy
and immaculate lawe.

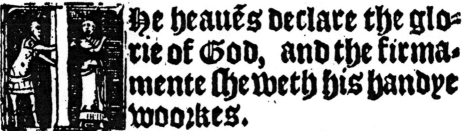

He heaues declare the glo=
rie of God, and the firma-
mente sheweth his handye
woorkes.

Daye vnto daie vttereth out speche, and night vnto night, openeth
knowledge.

There bee neither speches nor languages, but that the voyces of theim
bee heard.

Theyr sound hath gone furthe in=
to all landes, and theyr wordes through the coastes of the round yearth.

He hath pighte his pauilion in the
sunne, and he is like a bridgrom commyng out of his chamber.

He shall reioyce as a giaunt to rûne
his course, his progresse is from the
high heauen.

B.j.   And

He shal receiue blessyng of the lord and mercye of God his sauior.

This is the generacion of theym that seke him, of them that seke the face of the God of Jacob.

Ye Princes open youre gates, and ye eternal gates ope your selfes, and the kyng of glory shall enter in.

Who is this same Kyng of glori? A strong lorde, and a mightie, a lorde mightie in battaill.

ye Princes ope your gates, and ye eternall gates open your selfes, and the kyng of glory shall entre in.

Who is this same Kyng of glorye?

The lord of powers, he is the king of glorye.

Glory be to the father, and to the. &c.

As it was in the beginnyng, and is now, and euer shalbe. &c. Amen.

The antheme,

Christe is of power, euer perfitely to saue thē that come vnto God by hym: and he liueth euer to make intercession for vs.

Our

Our father which art in heaue. &c
And leade vs not into temptacion.
But deliuer vs from euill.

The blessyng.

The euerlastyng father blesse vs
wyth his blessyng euerlastyng. Ame.

The first lesson.

A Rod shall come forth of the
stocke of Iesse, and a blossome
shall florishe out of his roote.
The spirit of the lord shall rest vpon
him, the spirit of wisedo & vnderstandyng, the spirit of counsail & stregth,
the spirit of knowledge & godlynesse,
and the spirit of the feare of the lorde
shall replenish hym. He shall not geue
setece by the sight of the iyes, neither
reproue by here say, but he shal iudge
the poore people bi iustice, & in equitie
shall he reproue for the meke people
of the yearth, he shall smite the yearth
wyth the roode of hys mouthe, and
with the spirite of his lippes shall he
kil the vngodly. Righteousnesse shalbe the girdle of his loynes, and fayth-

B.iij.   fulnesse

culies the buearll of his reines.
Thus saieth the lorde turne vnto life
and ye shalbe saued.

The blessyng.

God the sonne of God vouchesafe to
blesse and succor vs.

The seconde lesson.

IN the moneth Gabriell was sent
fro God into a citie of Galile
named Nazareth, to a virgin
whiche was insured to a man, whose
name was Ioseph, of the house of
Dauid, and the Virgyns name was
Mary. And whē the angell came vn=
to her, he said: Haile full of grace, the
lorde is wyth the, Blessed art thou a=
mong women. And when the virgin
hearyng these wordes was troubled
with theim, and mused with her selfe
what maner of salutacion it should be
the angell said to her. Feare not Ma=
rie, be not abashed, for thou hast found
fauour in the sight of God. Lo, thou
shalt conceiue in thy wombe, and shalt
bryng furthe a sonne, and thou shalte
cal=

cal his name Jesus, he shalbe great &
shalbe called the sonne of the highest,
and the lorde shall geue vnto him the
seat of Dauid his father. And he shal
reigne ouer the house of Jacob for e-
uer, & his kyngdom shall haue no ende.
Thus sayeth the lorde: Turne vnto
me, and ye shalbe saued.

The grace of the holy ghost illumine
vs in harte and body.

Hen saied Mary to the an-
gel, how may this be done:
For I haue not knowledge
of man. And the angell an-
sweryng, sayed vnto her. The holy
ghost shall come frō aboue into thee
and the power of the highest shall o-
uershadowe thee. And therefore that
holy one that shalbee borne of thee,
shalbee called the sonne of God. And
lo, thy cosin Elizabeth, hath also conceiued a sonne in her old age, and this
is the sixt moneth sich she conceiued,
whiche

whiche was called the barrein woman, for there is nothyng impossible
to God: To this Mary answered, lo,
I am the handmaide of our lorde, be
it doen vnto me as thou hast spoken.

Thus saieth the lord: Turne vnto
me, and ye shalbe saued.

Te deum laudamus,

The praise of God, the father, the
sonne, and the holy ghost.

WE prayse thee O God, wee
knowledge thee to bee the
Lorde.

All the yearth doth wor-
ship thee, the father euerlastyng.

To the al angelles crie a loude, the
heauens and all powers therin.

To thee Cherubin and Seraphin
continually do crie.

Holy. Holy. Holy. Lorde God of Sa-
baoth.

Heauen and yearthe: are full of the
maiestie of thy glory.

The glorious company of the Apostles, prayse thee.

The

The goodlye felowſhip of the pro=
phetes, prayſe the.

The noble army of martyrs praiſe
the.

The holy Churche through out al
the world doth knowledge the.

The father of an infinite maieſtie.

Thy honorable, true, & onely ſon.

Alſo the holy goſt the comforter.

Thou arte the kynge of glorye, O
Chriſt.

Thou art the euerlaſtyng ſonne of
the father.

When thou tookeſt vpon thee to
deliuer man, thou diddeſt not abhorre
the virgyns wombe.

When thou haddeſt ouercome the
ſharpenes of death, thou dyddeſt opē
the kingdom of heauē to al beleuers.

Thou ſytteſt on the right hande of
God in the glory of the father.

We beleue that thou ſhalt come
too be our iudge.

We therefore praye the helpe thy
ſeruautes, whome thou haſt redemed

with thy precious bloud.

Make them to be numbred with thy sainctes in glory euerlastyng.

O lorde saue thy people, and blesse thyne herytage.

Gouerne them, and lyfte them vp for euer.

Day by day we magnyfie the.

And we worshype thy name, euer world without ende.

Uouchsafe O lord, to kepe vs this day without synne.

O Lord, haue merci vpon vs, haue mercy vpon vs.

O Lord, let thy mercy lighte vpon vs, as our trust is in the.

O lorde, in thee haue I trusted, let me neuer be confounded.

The Uersicle.

Pray for vs holy mother of God.

The Answere.

That we be made worthy to atteyne the promises of Christ.

O God

 GOD, to helpe me make good spede.

Lord make hast to succour me.

Glory be to the father, and to the sonne. &c.

As it was in the begynnyng, and is now, and euer shalbe. &c.

Deus miseriatur nostri. Psal. lxvi.

A prayer for the fauour and knowledge of God, and that his prayse may be spred thoroughout all the worlde.

GOd haue mercy vpon vs, and be good vnto vs, he shewe vs his bryght countenaūce, and haue mercy vpon vs.

That we may knowe thy waye in yearth, and thy sauyng helth emonge all nations.

Let the people magnifie the O God let all the people magnifie the.

Let the people be glad and ioyfull, because thou rulest the people wyth equity, also doest ordre the nacions in yearth.

C.ij.   Let

Let the people magnify þ, O God let al the people magnify the, the earth hath brought furth her fruite.

God our god blesse vs, God blesse vs, and all the coastes of the yearthe feare hym.

Glory be to the father. &c.
As it was in the beginnyng. &c. Am

Benedicite omnia opera. Daniel. iii.
The song of the thre childzen, wherwith they prayſed God walkyng in the fyze

Prayse ye the lorde, all the workes of the lorde prayse and exalt hym for euer.

The aungelles of the lord, prayse ye the lorde: ye heauens prayse the lorde.

Ye waters, al that are aboue heauē, prayse the lorde: al the powers of the Lorde, prayse ye the Lorde.

The sunne and moone, prayse ye the Lorde, sterres of the firmament prayse ye the lorde.

The rayne and the dewe prayse ye the

the lord, all the wyndes of god prayse
ye the lorde.

Fyre and heat, prayse ye the lorde,
wynter & sommer praise ye the lorde.

Dewes and hoare frostes, prayse
ye the lorde, frost and colde prayse ye
the lorde.

yse and snow, prayse ye the lorde,
nightes and daies prayse ye the lord.

Light and darknesse, prayse ye the
lorde, lightnyng and cloudes, prayse
ye the lorde.

The yearth prayse the lorde, laude
and exalte hym for euer.

Mountaynes and hylles, prayse ye
the lorde, all that springeth vpon the
yearth, prayse ye the lorde.

ye welles & springes, prayse ye the
lord, seas & fluddes, praise ye the lord.

Great fishes & all that moue in the
waters, prayse ye the lorde, all birdes
of the ayre prayse ye the lorde.

All beastes and cattall, prayse ye
the lorde: ye children of men, prayse ye
the lorde.

C.iij.   Let

Let Israell prayse the lorde, laude hym, and exalt hym for euermore.

Ye priestes of the lorde, prayse the lorde: ye seruauntes of the lord, praise the lorde.

Ye spirites and soules of rightwise men, prayse the lord, ye holy and meke in hart, prayse the Lorde.

Anania, Azaria, Misaell, praise ye the lord, laude and exalt him for euermore.

Blesse we the father, the sonne, and the holy gost: praise we him and exalt hym for euermore.

Blessed art thou lord in the firmament of heauen: thou art prayse worthy, glorious, & exalted, world without ende.

Laudate dominum de coelis. Psal. clxviii.

¶ All creatures are prouoked to the prayse of God.

Rayse the lorde ye that be in the heauens, praise ye him in the high places.

Praise

Praise ye hym al his angelles, al his powers prayse ye hym.

Praise ye him sunne and moone, al sterres and lyght prayse ye hym.

O heauens of heaues praise ye him and the waters aboue heauen, prayse the name of the lorde.

For by his worde all thynges were made, by his commaundemete al thynges were created.

He hath stablished them euerlastingly he hath set a lawe that shal not passe.

Praise the lord ye that be of ẙ yearth dragons and all the depe places.

Fyre, hayle, snowe, yse, stormes of windes, that do his commaundemet.

Mountaines and al litle hilles, trees bearyng frupte and all Cedres,

Bestes and al maner of cattail, serpentes, and all fethered foules.

Kynges of the yearthe & all people princes and all iudges of the yearth.

Youth and virgins olde and yonge, let them prayse the name of the lorde: for the name of hym only is exalted.

The

The prayse of him is aboue heauē
and yearth, and he hath exalted the
myght of hys people.

He be praised in al his saintes, son=
nes of Israel, the people approchyng
vnto hym.

The Antheme.

O wonderful exchaunge, the crea=
tour of mankynde takyng vpon
hym a liuyng bodye, hath not disday=
ned to be borne of a virgyn and he be=
yng made man without sede of man,
hath graunted vnto vs his godhead.

¶ The Chapiter. Maria virgo semper &c.

Virgin Mary, reioyce alwaye,
whiche hast borne Christe the
maker of heauen and earth: For out
of thy wombe thou hast brought fur=
th the sauiour of the world. Thākes
be to God.

The Hymne. Ales diei nuncius.

The byrde of day messinger,
Croweth & sheweth, that
lyght is here.

Chryst ý styrrer of the hart,
woylde

woulde we shoulde to lyfe conuert.

Upon Jesus let vs cry,
wepyng, praiyng, soberly,
Deuout prayer, meant with wepe,
Suffereth not oure hart to slepe.

Christ shake of our heauy slepe,
Breake the bondes, of nyght so depe,
Oure olde synnes clense and scoure,
Lyfe and grace, into vs powre.

¶ The song of zacharye.   Benedictus
¶ Thankes geuyng for the perfourmaunce
of Gods promise.

Lessed be the lorde God of
Israell, for he hath visited
and redemed his people.
And hath lifted vp the hor-
ne of saluation to vs, in the
house of his seruaunt Dauid.

As he spake bi the mouth of his ho
ly Prophetes, whiche hath been syns
the world began.

That we should be saued from our
enemies, and from the handes of all
that hate vs.

To perfourme the mercy promised

D.i.   to

to our fathers, and to remembre his holy couenaunt.

To perfourme the othe whiche he sware to oure father Abraham, that he woulo geue vs.

That we beyng deliuered out of the handes of our enemies, myght serue hym without feare.

In holinesse and righteousnesse before him, all the dayes of our lyfe.

And thou chylo, shalt be called the Prophet of the hyghest, for thou shalt go before the face of the Lord, to prepare his wayes.

To geue knoweledge of saluation vnto his people, for the remission of their synnes.

Through the tendre mercye of our god, wherby the day spryng from an hygh hath visited vs.

To geue light to them that sytte in darkenes and in the shadow of death and to guyde our fete into the way of peace.

Glory be to the father. &c.

The Collectes.

As it was in the begin. &c. Amen.

The Antheme.

BLessed be they, that heare the word of god, & kepe thesame.

The versicle.

O lord shewe thy mercy vnto vs.

The answere.

And geue to vs thy saluation.

Let vs pray.

GRaunt we beseche the lord God that thy seruauntes may enioy continuall helthe of bodye and soule. And that (the gracious virgyn Mari praiyng for vs) we may be delyuered from this present heuines, and haue the fruition of eternall gladnesse. Through Christ our lord. Amen.

Of the holy ghost.

Come holy spirit of god, inspire the hartes of them that beleue in the, and kyndle in them the fyre of thy loue.

Let vs pray

O God whiche by the information of the holy ghost, hast instructed

the hartes of thy faythfull, graunt vs
in the same spirit to haue right vnderstandyng , and euermore to reioyce in
his holy consolation. Through Chryst
our lord. Amen.

¶ Of the holy Trinite.

Delyuer vs, saue vs, iustifye vs, O
blessed Trinite.

Let vs pray.

ALmighti and euerlasting god
which hast graunted to vs thi
seruauntes by confession of the true
faith for to acknowledge the glory of
the eternal trinitie, and to honour the
one God in thy almightye maiestye:
we beseche thee, that throughe sted-
fastnesse in the same fayth, wee maye
be alway defended from al aduersitie
whiche lyuest and reignest one God
worlde without ende. Amen.

¶ Of the Crosse of Christ.

We oughte to glory in the Crosse of
our Lord Jesus Christ.

Let vs pray.

O God , whiche hast ascended thy
most

most holy Crosse, and hast geuē lyght
to the darknesse of the world, vouch=
safe to illumyne , visyt and comfort
both our hartes and bodyes, whiche
lyuest and reignest God, world with=
out ende. Amen.

¶ Of the holy Apostles.
ye be they that haue left all thynges
and haue folowed me, ye shal receiue
an hūdred fold, & haue the possession
of euerlastyng lyfe.

¶ Let vs pray.
ALmightie God, regard our in=
firmitie, and for that the bur=
den of oure iniquitie oppresseth vs:
Graunte that by the prayer of thy glo
rious Apostles, we may haue reliefe
and strength to folowe the confession
of their faith.   Through Christe
our Lorde. Amen.

¶ Of the holy Martyrs.
The soules of sainctes reioyse in hea=
uen, which haue folowed the steppes
of Christ, and because they haue shed
theyr blod for his loue, therefore shall
                    D.iij.   thei

they reigne with Christ for euer.

Let vs pray.

ORaunt to vs almightye God, that we which knowe that thy glorious Martyrs wer strong in confession of thy fayth, may haue the ioy of their felowship in euerlasting gladnesse. Through Christ our lord. Am̄.

For peace.

Lord send vs peace in our daies, for there is none other that fyghteth for vs, but onely thou O lord god.

Let vs pray.

O God from whome all holy desyres, all good counsels, and all iust workes do procede, geue vnto thy seruauntes that same peace, whiche the world cannot geue, that our hartes beyng obedient to thy commaundementes, and the feare of our ennemyes taken away, oure tyme may be peaceable by thy protectiō. Through Christ our lord. amen.

A prayer of the passion.
Christ suffered for vs, leuyng vs example

exāple that we shuld folowe his steppes who dyd no synne, neyther was ther any gyle found in his mouth.

The versicle.

We worshyp the Chryst, with prayse and benediction.

The answere.

For thou hast redemed the worlde from endlesse affliction.

Let vs praye.

LOrde Iesu Chrst. sonne of the liuing god, set thy holy passiō crosse and death, betwene thy iudgement & our soules both now & at the houre of death. And moreouer vouchsafe to graunt vnto the liuyng mercye and grace, to the dead pardō and rest to thy holi church peace and concord, and to vs wretched synners lyfe and ioy euerlasting: which liuest and reignest God with the father and the holi gost world without ende. Amen.

The glorious passion of our lord Iesu Chrst., deliuer vs from sorowfull heuinesse, and bring vs to the ioyes of Paradise. Amen.   The

they reigne with Christ for euer.

Let vs pray.

ORaunt to vs almightye God, that we which knowe that thy glorious Martyrs wer strong in confession of thy fayth, may haue the ioy of their felowship in euerlasting gladnesse. Through Christ our lord. Amē.

For peace.

Lord send vs peace in our daies, for there is none other that fyghteth for vs, but onely thou O lord god.

Let vs pray.

O God from whome all holy desyres, all good counsels, and all iust workes do procede, geue vnto thy seruauntes that same peace, whiche the world cannot geue, that our hartes beyng obedient to thy commaundementes, and the feare of our ennemyes taken away, oure tyme may be peaceable by thy protectiō. Through Christ our lord. amen.

A prayer of the passion.

CHrist suffered for vs, leuyng vs example

exãple that we shuld folowe his steppes who dyd no synne , neyther was ther any gyle found in his mouth.

✢ The versicle.

We worshyp the Chryst, with prayse and benediction.

The answere.

For thou hast redemed the worlde from endlesse affliction.

✢ Let vs praye.

LOrde Jesu Christ. sonne of the liuing god, set thy holy Passiõ crosse and death, betweue thy iudgement & our soules both now & at the houre of death. And moreouer vouch safe to graunt vnto the liuyng mercye and grace, to the dead pardõ and rest to thy holi church peace and concord, and to vs wretched synners lyfe and ioy euerlasting: which liuest and reig= nest God with the father and the holi gost world without ende. Amen.

The glorious passion of our lord Je= su Christ., deliuer vs from sorowfull heuinesse, and bring vs to the ioyes of paradise. Amen,   The

O God to helpe me make good spede.

Lorde make hast to succoure me.

Glory be to the father and to the sonne. &c

As it was in the begynnyng, and is nowe, and euer shalbe world without ende. Amen

¶ The Hymne

Flowe of thy fathers lyght, Lyght of light and day most bryght,

Christ that chasest away nyghte, Ayde vs for to pray aright.

Driue out Darknes, frō our mides Driue away the flocke of fendes, Drousynes, take from our eyes, That from slouth we may aryse, Christ vouchsafe mercy to geue, To vs all that do beleue, Let it profit vs that pray, All that we do syng or say. Amen.

Con-

Confitemini domino, Pfal, cxvii

All men are prouoked to magnifie
and pzayse the Lozde God.

Rayse the Lozde foz he is
good, foz his mercy is euer=
lastyng.

Let Israel saie now that
he is good, foz his mercye is euerla=
styng

Let the house of Aaron say nowe,
that his mercy is euerlastyng.

Let al that feare the lozd, say now,
that his mercy is euerlastyng.

In my trouble J called vpõ the lozd
and the lozd hath harde me at large.

The lozde is my helper, J will not
feare what man doth to me.

The lozd is my helper, and J shal
despise myne enemies.

Better it is to trust in the lozd, then
to trust in man.

Better it is to trust in the Lozde,
then to trust in Pzinces.

Al natiõs haue compassed me, yet
in the Lozdes name haue J vanqui=

E.j.   shed

ched theim.

Thei liyng in wait haue closed me in, yet in the Lordes name haue I vanquished theim.

Thei haue swarmed about me like bees, and thei haue burnte me as fire amõg thornes, yet in the lordes name haue I vanquished theim.

I was thrust at with violence redi to fall, and the lord succoured me.

My strength and praise is the lord and he is made my saluacion.

The voyce of reioysyng and helth, is in the tabernacles of the iuste.

The Lordes righte hande hath wroughte the strengthe, the Lordes righte hande hath exalted me: The lordes right hande hath wrought the strengthe.

I shal not dye but I shall liue and I shall shewe the workes of the lord.

The lord hath chasted and chasted me, and hath not put me to death.

Open me ye gates of righteousnes and I enteryng thereby shall praise the

the lorde, this is the Lordes gate, the righteous shall entre therby.

I wil praise thee O lorde (because thou hast heard me) and thou art become my saluacion.

The stone which the buylders cast awaie, is made the hedd stone of the corner.

This is doen bi the lord, and it is marueilous in oure eies.

This is the day, which the Lord made, let vs reioyse ⁊ be meri therin.

O lord saue thou me, O lord make me prospere, blessed is he that commeth in the lordes name.

We haue blessed you, that be of the lordes house, God is the Lorde, and hath geuen lighte vnto vs.

Appointe ye a solempne holy day, decked with bowes, to the corner of the aulter.

Thou art my God, and I shal rendre thankes to thee: thou art my God and I shall exalt the.

I shal praise the, O lorde for thou

E.ii.   hast

haste harde me, and arte become my
saluacion.

Pꝛayse the loꝛde: foꝛ he is good, foꝛ
his mercy is euerlastyng.

Gloꝛy be to the father. &c.

As it was in the. &c.

The antheme.

BLessed are the pooꝛe in spyꝛit,
foꝛ theirs is the kyngdome of
heauen: Blessed are thei that mourne
foꝛ thei shal receiue comfoꝛt.

The versicle.

Loꝛde heare my pꝛayer.

The aunswere

And let my cry come to thee.

Let vs pꝛay.

LOrd Iesu Chꝛist most pooꝛe
and mylde of spirit, whiche
diddest mourne and lamente
foꝛ our synnes and infidelitie: graunt
vs likewise to be pooꝛe and mylde of
spirit & so to wepe and wayle foꝛ our
offeces, that we maie be parteners of
thy heauely kingdome, which liuest &
reignest god woꝛld wihtout end. Am

The

The third houre.

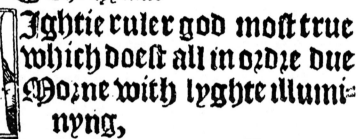

God, to helpe me make good spede.

Lorde make haste to succor me.

Glory be to the father, and to the sonne. &c.

As it was in the beginnyng and is now, and euer shalbe. &c. Amen.

¶ The Hymne

Ightie ruler god most true
which doest all in ordre due
Morne with lyghte illumi-
nyng,
Nonetide with heate garnishyng.

Quenche the flames of our debate,
Foule and noysome heate abate:
Graunt vnto our bodies health,
To our hartes true peace & wealth.

Let tong and harte strégth & sence,
Commende thy magnificence:
Let thy spirite of charitie,
Stirre vs al to worship thee. Amen.

Ad dominum cum. psal, cxix
A prayer to bee deliured from
the vanitie of the worlde.

E.iij.　I

I Cryed vnto the lorde when I was in trouble, and he hath hearde me.

O lord, deliuer my soule from liyng lippes, and a deceiptfull tongue.

What maie bee geuen thee, or what maie bee put to thee against a deceiptefull toungue.

It is like sharpe arrowes of the mightie man, & hote burnyng cooles.

Wo is me that my restyng place is prolonged, I haue dwelled with the inhabitātes of Cedar: my soule hath been long in exile.

I was at peace with theim that hated peace: when I spake vnto theim, thei assaulted me without cause.

Glory be to the father, and to. &c.

As it was in the begin. &c. Amen.

The Antheme.

B Lessed are the meke, for thei shal inherite the yearth. Blessed are thei whiche suffre hunger and thyrste for ryghteousnes, for thei

thei shalbe satisfied.

The versicle

Lorde heare my prayer.

The aunswere

And let my cry come to thee.

Let vs pray.

LOrde Jesu Christ whose whole lyfe was nothyng but humilitie and mekenesse, who only art our very righteousnes: Graunte vs to serue and honor the with humble and meke hart, and in all our life and conuersacion to desire to bee occupied in the woorkes of righteousnesse: which liuest and reignest God world without end. Amen.

The sixt houre.

O GOD, to helpe me make good spede.

Lorde make haste to succor me.

Glory be to the father. &c.

As it was in t he begynnyng, and is now, and euer shalbe. &c. Amen.

The

The hympne.

O Creatoz moste benigne,
To vs alway be lokyng,
Raise vs from all noysome
      slepe,
wherein we bee drouned depe.
      Christe of thy mercifulnesse:
Pardon all our sinfulnesse,
Thee to praise and magnifie,
Of night we leaue the slogardy.
      Of the synne that we haue doen,
we make our confession,
wepyng we do pray to thee,
Pardon our iniquitie.

      Ad te leuaui oculos meos, psal, xxii
            A prayer to bee deliuered from
                  the skornes of the wicked.

I Haue lifte vp myne iyes to
thee, whiche dwelleste in
heauen.
      Beholde, euen like as the
iyes of the seruauntes wayte at their
Masters handes.
      As the iyes of the handmaide be v-
pon her maistresse: euen so bee oure
                                                iyes

iyes vpon our lorde God, vntyll he haue mercy vpon vs.

Haue mercy on vs O Lorde, haue mercy on vs, for we be had in muche contempt.

For our soule is very ful, being skorned of the ryche and dyspysed of the proude.

Glory be to the father, & to the. &c.

As it was in the begin. &c. Amen.

℟ The Antheme.

BLessed are the mercifull, for they shall get mercie. Blessed are the cleane in harte, for they shall se God.

The versycle.

Lorde heare my prayer.

The aunswere.

And let my crie come to the.

℟ Let vs praye.

LOrde Jesu Christe, whose propertie is to be mercyfull, whyche arte alwaye pure and cleane vythout spotte of synne: Graunt vs thy grace to folowe thee in mercyfulnesse towarde

our neighbours, and alwaies to beare
a pure harte and a cleane conscience
towardes the, that we may after this
lyfe se the in thy euerlastyng glory:
which liuest and reignest God worlde
without ende. Amen.

❡ The Nynth houre.

God to helpe me make
good spede.
Lorde make hast to suc-
cour me.
Glory be to the father, ⁊
to the sonne, and to the holy ghost.

As it was in the beginning and is
nowe, and euer shalbe. ⁊c. Amen.

❡ The hympne.

The glory eternall.
Blessed hope of men mor-
tall.
Christ the sonne of God
on high.
The sonne of virgin Mary.
Reche thy hand that we may ryse.
And our mindes so exercise.

That

That deuoutely we may syng.

Paise of God with thankesgeuing.

Finally, O Christ we craue.

Faythe in our hartes set and graue,

That through hope of life aboue,

We maie flame with feruent loue. Amen.

Domine quis habitabit. Psalm. xiiii.

The innocent liuer shall entre
into euerlasting lyfe.

LOrd who shall dwell in thy
tabernacle? Or who shall
rest in thy holy hyll?

He that entreth without
spot, and worketh righteousnesse: he
that speaketh truthe in his hart, and
hath not vsed deceipt in his toungue.

Nor hath done any euil to his neigh=
bour, and hath not slaundered his neigh=
bour.

He in whose syght the wicked man
is nothing regarded, but doth honour
theim that feare the lorde.

He that sweareth to his neighbour,
and deceiueth hym not: he that hath
not laid his money to vsury nor hath

F. ii.   not

nor receyued rewardes agaynste the
innocent.

He that doeth these thinges, shal ne=
uer stagger nor decaie.

The Antheme.

BLessed are ý peace makers, for
thei shalbe called the children of
God. Blessed are they that suffre per=
secucion for ryghteousnesse sake, for
theirs is the kingdome of heauen.

The versycle.

Lorde heare my praier.

The aunswere.

And let my cry come to the.

Let vs praie.

LOrde Iesu Christ, which ma=
dest peace betwene God the
father and vs miserable syn=
ners, whiche notwithstandyng dyd
dest suffre iniustly, iniuries and perse=
cucions: graunt vs grace to kepe the
peace that thou hast made, and paci=
ently to beare all iniuries & persecuci=
ons, that we may bee called thy chyl=
dren, inherite thy heauenly kyngdõ
whiche liuest and raignest.&c. Amen.

The

The euensong.

 God to helpe me make good spede.

Lorde make hast to succour me.

Glory be to the father, ꝗ to the sonne, and to the holy ghost.

As it was in the beginning and is nowe, and euer shalbe, worlde without ende. Amen.

Laudate pueri dominum. Psalm. cxii.

Here we be stirred to prayse and magnifie the Lorde.

Raise the Lorde, O ye children, prayse ye the name of the lorde.

Blessed be the name of the lorde, from this tyme furth, and euer more.

The Lordes name be praised, from the East vnto the west.

The lord is high, aboue all nacions and his glorie aboue the heauens.

Who is like vnto the lord our God that hath his dwellyng on hyghe:

F.iij.   and

and yet humbleth himſelfe to behold the thiges that are in heauen & yearth

He rayſeth vp the ſymple out of the duſt, and lyfteth the pooꝛe out of the myꝛe.

That he may ſet him with the prin-ces, euē with the princes of ẏ people.

He maketh the barren woman to ke pe houſe, and to bee a ioyful mother of childꝛen.

Gloꝛy be to the father, and to. &c.

As it was in the begin. &c. Amen.

Laudate nomen dom.ni. Pſalm.cxxxiiii.

God is to be pꝛayſed foꝛ his maruei-lous woꝛkes and benefites.

Rayſe ye the name of the loꝛd O ye ſeruaūtes, praiſe the loꝛde.

ye that ſtande in the houſe of the Loꝛd, in the courtes of the hou-ſe of our God.

O pꝛayſe the loꝛde, foꝛ the Loꝛde is gracious, O ſyng prayſes vnto his na-me, foꝛ it is louely.

Foꝛ the Loꝛde hath choſen Jacob vnto

vnto himſelfe, and Iſrael foz his awn poſſeſſion.

Foz I know that the lozde is great and that our lozd is aboue al Goddes.

The Lozde hath done all thynges that he would, in heauen & in yearth and in the ſea, and in all depe places.

He bzingeth furth the cloudes from the endes of the wozlde, and turneth the lightenynges into rayne: he bzyn= geth furthe the wyndes out of theyz places.

He ſmote the firſte bozne of Egypte both of man and beaſt.

He hath ſent tokens and wonders into the middeſt of the, O lande of Egypt, vpon Pharao and all hys ſer= uauntes.

He ſmote diuerſe nacions, and ſlew mightie kynges.

Seon kyng of the Amozites, and Og the kyng of Baſan, & all the kyng= domes of Canaan.

And gaue their lande in herytage, in herytage to Iſraell his people.

Thȝ

Thy name O Lorde, endureth for euer, O Lorde thy memoriall is from generacion to generacion.

For the lorde wyll reuenge his people, & be gracious vnto his ſeruauntes

As for the Idolles of the Heathen they are but ſyluer & gold, the woorke of mens handes.

Thei haue mouthes and ſpeake not they haue eyes and ſe not.

They haue eares and heare not, neither is there any breath in their mouthes.

They that make them, be like vnto them, and ſo are all they that put their truſte in them.

Prayſe the lord, the houſe of Iſrael, prayſe the lorde, the houſe of Leui, ye that feare the lorde, prayſe the lord.

Prayſed be the lord of Syon, which dwelleth at Ieruſalem.

Glory be to the father, & to the ſonne and to the holy ghoſt.

As it was in the beginning, and is now, and euer ſhalbe. &c. Amen.

Con-

The evensong.

Confitebor tibi. pſalm. cxxxvii.

¶ A pzaiſe and thankeſgeuing vnto God.

I Wyll geue thankes to the, O lozd, with my whole hart.

Befoze thy aungels I wyll ſyng to the : I wyll woꝛſhyp toward thy holy temple, and pzayſe thy name.

Becauſe of thy mercye and truthe, foz thou haſt magnified thy name a=boue all thinges.

Whenſoeuer I call vpon the, heare me, thou ſhalt endue my ſoule wyth muche ſtrength.

All the kynges of the yearth, pzaiſe the O lozd, foz they haue heard all the woꝛdes of thy mouth.

And let them ſyng in the wayes of the Loꝛde, foz great is the gloꝛy of the Loꝛde.

Foz though the Loꝛde be hygh, yet hath he reſpecte vnto the lowely, ꝗ as foz the pzoud he beholdeth thē afar of.

Though I walke in the middeſt of trouble, yet ſhalt thou refreſhe me,

ℭ.i.

thou shalt stretche furth thyne hande vpon the furiousnes of mine enemies and thy right hand shall saue me.

The lorde shall make good for me, thy mercy O lorde endureth for euer, dispyse not then the workes of thyne owne handes.

Glory be to the father, & to the. &c.

℣ The Antheme.

BLessed be the name of the lorde for euermore.

The Chapiter.

BLessed art thou, O virgin Mary, whiche hast borne our lorde the creator of the worlde, thou haste brought furth him that madethe, and alwaies remainest a virgin.

℣ The hymne.

OLord the worldes sauiour, whiche haste preserued vs this daie.

This night also be our succour, and saue vs euer we the pray.

Be mercifull now vnto vs.

And

And spare vs, which do pray to the,
Our synne forgeue lorde gracious.

And our darknes, mought lightened be.

That slepe, our myndes do not oppresse.

Nor that our enemy, vs begile.
For that flesh, full of fraylenes.
Our soule and body, do defyle.
O lord, refourmer of all thing.
with hartes desyre, we pray to the.
That after our rest and sleping, we
may ryse chaste, and worshyp the.
Amen.

℘The versicle.

Blessed is Mary, amonges al womē.

℘The answere.

And blessed is the fruit of her wombe

Magnificat anima mea. &c.

℘The song of Mary retoysyng and pray
syng the goodnes of God.

y soule doeth magnifie the
Lorde.

And my spiritte hath re-
ioysed in God my sauiour.

G. ij.   F. ij.

For he hathe regarded the lowly-
neſſe of his handmayden.

For behold, from hencefurth all generacions ſhall call me bleſſed.

For he that is mighty, hath magnified me, and holy is his name.

And his mercy is on them that fear
hym, throughout all generacions.

He hath ſhewed ſtrength with hys
arme, he hath ſcattered the proude in
the imagination of their hartes.

He hath put downe the mighty frō
their ſtate, and hath exalted the humble and meke.

He hath fylled the hungery wyth
good thynges, and the ryche he hath
ſent emptie awaye.

He remembryng his mercie, hathe
holpen his ſeruaunt Iſrael, as he pro-
myſed to our fathers, Abraham and
his ſeede for euer.

Glory be to the father, & to the ſonne
and to the holy ghoſt.

As it was in the beginning, and is
now, & euer ſhalbe. &c. Amen.

¶ The

The euensong.

¶The Antheme.

NO, all thinges be fulfylled that were spoken of the Aungell by the virgin Mari. Thankes be to God.

¶The versicle.

Lord heare my praier.

¶The Aunswere.

And let my cry come to the.

¶Let vs praye.

HOly Lorde, almightie father, euerlasting God, whiche dyddest replenysh the blessed virgin Mary, with moste plentiful grace, and spirituall giftes, wherby she praysed and magnified the: Graunt that thy holy ghost may with lyke grace and inspiracion, kyndle our hartes, to sanctifie thy holy name: Through Christ our Lorde. Amen.

¶The Complyn.

Onuert vs God our sauiour.

And turne thy wrath away from vs.

O God, to helpe me

make good spede.

Lord make haste to succour me.

Glory be to the father, & to the sonne and to the holy ghost.

As it was in the beginning, and is nowe, and euer shalbe, worlde without ende. Amen.

Vsque quo demine. Psal. xii.
A praier against tempt\-
tacion.

Owe long wilt thou forget me, O Lord, for euer: howe long wilt thou turne thy face from me?

Howe long shall I haue troublous thoughtes in my soule, and heauinesse in my hart, day by day?

Howe long shall myne enemy be ex\-alted ouer me? behold and heare me, O lorde my God.

Illumine mine iyes, lest I slepe any tyme in death: and that mine enemy neuer say, I haue preuayled agaynst hym.

They that trouble me, wyll reioyce

if J be cast doune, but J haue trusted in thy mercy.

Myne hart shall reioyce in thy saluacion, J shal syng to the lord that geueth me great benefites, and J shall praise the name of the lord most high.

Glory be to the father, and.&c.

As it was in the begin.&c. Amen.

Iudica me deus.Psalm.xlii.

¶A prayer to be deliuered from our aduersaries that we may syng the praise of God.

Iudge on my syde, O God, defende my cause against the vnholy people : from the vniust and deceitful mā deliuer me.

Fo thou O God, art my strength, why hast thou put me away: why goo J so heauely, whilest mine enemy vexeth me.

Send furth thy light and thy truth they haue led me, and brought me into thy holy hyl, & thy dwelling places.

And J shall entre vnto the aultar of GOD, vnto God that maketh my youth

youth to reioyce.

I shal praise the with harpe, O god my God, why arte thou heuy O my soule: & why doest thou trouble me.

Trust in God, for yet shall I prayse hym, he is the helth of my countenauce and my God.

Glory be to the father, & to the sonne and to the holy ghost.

As it was in the beginning. &c.

℞ The Antheme.

Aue vs good lord waking, and kepe vs slepyng, that we may wake in Christ, and rest in peace.

The Chapiter.

Thou art (O Lorde) in the middest of vs: and inuocatiō of thy name is made ouer vs, forsake vs not, O lorde our God.

℞ The hymne.

Lord the maker of all thyng, we praye the now in this euenyng.

Us to defende, through thy mercie.

From all deceit of our enemy.

Let neither vs deluded be.

Good lord, with dreame or phantasy,

Our hart wakyng in thee thou kepe.

That we in synne fall not on slepe.

O father through thy blessed sonne.

Graunt vs this our peticion.

To whō with ÿ holy ghost al waies,

In heauen and yearth bee laude and
prayse. Amen.

¶ The versicle.

Behold the handmaide of the Lorde.

¶ The Aunswere.

Be it done to me accordyng too thy
worde.

Nunc dimittis. Luc. i.

¶ The song of Symeon the iust.

Lorde, nowe lettest thou thy
seruaunt depart in peace according to thy worde.

For myne iyes haue sene
thy saluacion.

Whiche thou hast prepared, before
the face of all thy people.

To be a light for to lighten the men

am withered amõg all mine enemies.

Auoide from me all ye, that worke wickednes, for the lorde hath hearde the voyce of my weping.

The lord hath heard my praier, the lord hath heard my peticion.

Let all myne enemyes be ashamed and confounded, let them be ashamed, and confounded very quickely.

Glory be to the father, and. &c.

As it was in the begin. &c. Amen.

Beati quorum Psalm. xxxi.

℄ Howe the penitent persone should bewaile his synnes, pray vnto God and reioyce in hym.

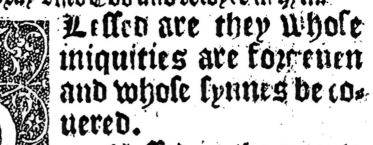

Lessed are they whose iniquities are forgeuen and whose synnes be couered.

Blessed is the man to whome God hath not imputed synne, and in whose spirite is not deceit.

For whylest I helde my peace, my bones are waxen olde: whilest I cried all the day.

For day and night thy hand is very

heauy vpon me : I haue bene turned
into wretchednesse whilest the thorne
pricked me.

I haue opened my faulte vnto the,
& haue not hid mine vnrighteousnes.

I said, I wyll confesse mine vnrighteousnes against my selfe to the lorde,
and thou hast forgeuē the wickednesse
of my synne.

For this shall euery holy persone
pray vnto the in tyme conuenient.

But in the greate fludde of many
waters, they shal not come nigh hym.

Thou art my refuge frō tribulatiō
that hath inclosed me: O my ioy delyuer me from them, that compasse me.

I shall geue the vnderstanding and
shall teache the in the way that thou
shalt go : I shal fastē my iyes vpō the.

Be ye not lyke Horse and Mule, in
whom is none vnderstandyng.

Bynde their mouthes with snaffle
and brydle, that will not drawe nygh
vnto the.

Many are the plagues of the sinner,

but whoso trusteth in the lorde, mercy
embraceth hym on euery syde.

Be glad in the lorde, and reioyce ye
ryghteous, and be ioyous al ye that be
vpzyght in hart.

Glozy be to the father, and.&c.
As it was in the begin.&c.Amen.

Domine ne, Psalm.xxxvii.

℡ The penitent presone soze greued with the bur=
den of synne,called vpon God foz ayde and
betaketh hymselfe to his mercy.

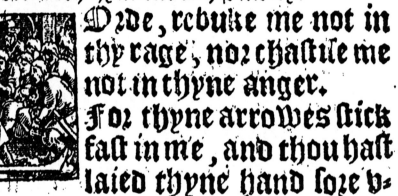Ozde, rebuke me not in
thy rage, noz chastise me
not in thyne anger.

For thyne arrowes stick
fast in me, and thou hast
laied thyne hand soze v-
pon me.

There is no health in my flesshe be=
cause of thy dyspleasure : there is no
rest in my bones, because of my sinnes.

For myne iniquities are gone ouer
mine hed,and are laied vpon me as an
heauy burden.

My woundes are putrified and rot-
ten,because of my folishnes.

I am made wretched and croked extreinely, I went sorowful al day lōg.

For my loynes are full of illusions, and there is no health in my fleash.

I am sore afflicted and brought low I dyd roare out for the sorowe of my hart.

Lorde, thou knowest all my desyre, and my mourning is not hid from the.

My harte is troubled, my strength hath left me, also the very syght of mine iyes is not with me.

My frendes and my neyghbours drewe together, and stode against me.

And they that were next me, stode farre of: they that laied waite for my lyfe, set vpon me.

And they that soughte my destruction, speake vanities, and they ymagined deceites all the day.

But I as one beyng deafe, dyd not heare, and I was as one that were domme, not openyng his mouth.

And I became as a man not hearyng, and hauyng no countercheckes in his mouth.

For in the haue I trusted, thou shalt heare me my lord God.

For I haue said, let neuer mine enemies triumphe vpon me, and whylest my feete do slyde, they spake stoutely agaynst me.

For I am ready to be scourged, and my sorowe is alwaies in my remembraunce.

For I shall confesse mine vngodlynesse, and shall thinke vpon my sinne.

But mine enemies lyue & are made strong ouer me, and they are increased, whiche hate me vniustly.

They that requyted euyll for good were against me, because I folowed goodnesse.

Forsake me not, O lord my God neither departe thou from me.

Make spede to helpe me, O Lorde God of my saluacion.

Glory be to the father, and to. &c.

As it was in the begin. &c. Amen.

Miserere mei deus. Psalm. l.

A praier of the penitent, earnestly acknowledging
and lamentyng his vngodly life, and cryng for
mercie to be clensed from synne, and callyng
for the Spirite of God to be confir=
med in grace.

Aue mercy vpon me, O
God, according to thy great
mercy.

And according to the mul=
titude of thy compassions, wype away
mine iniquitie.

More and more wash me from mine
iniquite, and clense me from my sinne.

For I knowlege myne iniquitie, &
my synne is euer before myne iyes.

To the alone haue I synned, & haue
done euill in thy syght, that thou ma=
yest be iustified in thy wordes, & maiest
ouercome when thou art iudged.

Behold, I was begotten in wicked=
nes, and my mother conceyued me in
synne.

Lo, thou hast loued truthe, the vn=
knowen and secret thinges of thy wis=
dome thou hast reueled vnto me.

Sprynkle me lord with Hysop, and

I shalbe clensed.

Thou shalt wasshe me, and I shall be made whytter then snowe.

Unto my hearing shalt thou geue ioye & gladnes, and the brused bones shall reioyce.

Turne thy face from my sinnes, and wype away all my wickednes.

A pure hart create in me, O GOD, and a perfite spirit renew within me.

Cast me not away from thy face, & thy holy spirit take not from me.

Restore to me the gladnes of thy saluacion, and strengthen me with the principall spirit.

I wil instruct the wicked in thy wayes, and the vngodly shalbe conuerted vnto the.

Deliuer me from bloudshed, O God, the God of my health, and my toung shall exalt thy righteousnes.

Thou shalt open my lippes, and my mouth shall shewe thy prayse.

For if thou hadcest desired sacrifice I had surely geuen it, but thou deligh=

test not in whole burnt offerynges.

The sacrifice to God is a lowly spirite, O God, thou wylt not despyse a contrite and an humble hart.

Deale gently of thy fauourable beneuolēce with Syon, that the walles of Ierusalem may be builded vp.

Then shalt thou accept the sacrifice of righteousnes, oblacions and whole burnt offerynges, then shall they laye calues vpon thyne aultar.

Glory be to the father, & to the sonne and to the holy ghost.

As it was in the beginning, and is now, and euer shalbe, worlde without ende. Amen.

Domine exaudi. psalm. ci.

A sore complaint of the Godly man, beyng greuously handled of the wicked people, and makyng his mone to almightie God.

Orde heare my praier, and let my crie come vnto the.

Turne not thy face from me, whetnsoeuer I am troubled, bowe thyne eare vnto me.

In what daie soeuer I cal vpon the heare me spedely.

For my daies are banished as smoke and my bones are waxed as drie as a fyre brande.

I am striken, and myne hart is wythered lyke haye, so that I haue forgotten to eate my breade.

With the noise of my mourning my bone cleaueth to my flesshe.

I am lyke vnto a Pellican of wyldernes, and lyke vnto an Owle in the house.

I haue waked, and am like a Sparowe solitary in the house toppe.

All daie myne enemies reuiled me, and they that praised me, conspired against me.

For I did eate asshes as bread, and myngeled my drinke with wepyng.

And that because of thy wrath and indignacion, for thou diddest take me vp and cast me against the ground.

My daies are faded as a shadowe, & I withered like haye.

But thou lorde abidest for euer, and thy memoriall is from age to age.

Thou Lorde shalt aryse and haue mercy of Syon, for it is tyme to haue mercy on it, for the tyme is come.

For the stones therof delighteth thy seruauntes, and they shall haue pitie on the grounde therof.

And the people shal feare thy name O lorde, and all kynges of the yearth thy glory.

For the Lorde hath builded Syon, and shalbe seen in his glory.

He hath regarded the speche of the humble, and hath not despysed their praier.

Let these thynges be wrytten in an other age, and the people that shalbe created shall prayse the lorde.

For he hath loked doune from hys high holy place, the lorde hath loked doune from heauen vnto the yearth.

To heare the wailyng of them that be captiue, to lose the sonnes of them that were slayn.

That they should in Syon declare the name of the Lorde, and his prayse in Hierusalem.

When the people assembled together, & kynges for to serue the lorde.

In the way he hath hyndered my strength, he hath shortened my daies.

Call me not away in the middes of my daies, thy yeres endure for euer.

In the beginning thou Lorde haste laied the foundacion of the yearth, and the woorkes of thyne handes are the heauens.

They shall perysh, but thou abidest and they shall all waxe olde as a garment.

And as a coueryng thou shalt chaunge theim, and they shalbe chaunged, but thou arte one, and the same, and thy yeres shall not fayle.

The sonnes of thy seruauntes shal continue, and their seede shall stande fast for euer.

Glory be to the father, & to the sonne and to the holy ghost.

As it was in the beginnin, and is
now, and euer shalbe, worlde with=
out ende. Amen.

Deprofundis clamaui. Psalm. cxxix

The synner beyng punyshed for his synnes,
desireth to be deliuered both from sinne
and punishment.

From the depth I called on
the (O Lorde) Lorde heare
my voice.

Let thine eares geue good
hede to the voyce of my praier.

If thou lord, wilt loke straightly v=
pon sinnes, O lord who shal abide it?

But with the is mercy, and for thy
lawe haue I suffered the, O lorde.

My soule hath abiden in his worde,
my soule hath trusted in the lorde.

From the mourning watche vnto
nigh, let Israel truste in the lorde.

For with the lorde there is mercy, &
with hym is plenteous redempcion.

And he will redeme Israel from al
his iniquities.

Glory be to the father, and to. &c.

The seuen Psalmes.

As it was in the begin. &c. Amen.

Dominc exaudi. Psalm. cxli.

The iust man beyng in aduersitie, prayeth
to be deliuered from all euill.

LOrde heare my praier, with
thine eares perceiue my desyre for thy truth sake, & hear
me for thy righteousnes.

And enter not into iudgement with
thy seruaunte, for no persone lyuyng
shalbe iustified in thy syght.

For the enemy hathe pursued my
soule, my life in yearth he hath brought lowe.

He hath set me in darkenesse as the
dedde men of the worlde, and my spy-
rite was vexed, my harte was troubled within me.

I remembred the olde daies, I haue
studied of all thy woorkes, and in the
deedes of thy handes I mused.

I haue stretched furthe my handes,
vnto the, my soule vnto the as yearth
without water.

Hastely heare me O lorde, my spirit

hath failed me

Turn not thy face frō me, for I shal be like vnto men descēding into a pit

Cause thy mercy to bee harde of me betymes, for in thee haue I trusted.

Shewe me the waie where I maye walke, for vnto thee haue I lyfte vp my mynde.

Deliuer me frō myne enemies lorde vnto thee I haue fled teache me to do thy will, for thou art my God.

Thy good spirite shall conducte me into the lande of rightfulnesse, for thy namesfake Lorde, thou shalt reuiue me through thy equety.

Thou shalt bring my soule frō troble, and through thy mercy thou shalt destroye al myne enemyes.

And thou shalt destroi al that molest my soule, for I am thy seruaunte.

Glory be to the father, & to the sonne ond to thee holy ghoste.

As it was in the beginning, and is now, and euer shalbe, worlde without ende. Amen.

B.i.   The

The anthem

Remembre not (O Lorde
GOD) our old iniquites
but lette thi mercie spedely
prevent vs, for we be veri
miserable: Helpe vs God our sauior,
and for the glory of thi name, deliuer
vs, bee merciful and forgeue our sinnes, for thy names sake. Let not the
wicked people say, whe are is there
God: We be thy people and the sheepe
of thy pasture, we shal geue thankes
to thee for euer, from age to age
we shall set furth thy laude
and praise. To thee bee
honour and glory
worlde with-
out ende
Amen.

The

The Letany.

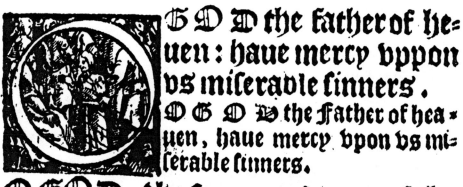

GOD the father of heuen : haue mercy vppon vs miserable sinners.

O GOD the Father of heauen, haue mercy vpon vs miserable sinners.

O GOD, the sonne, redemer of the worlde : haue mercy vpon vs miserable sinners.

O GOD, the sonne, redemer of the worlde &

O God, the holy ghoste, proceding from the father and the sonne : haue mercy vpon vs miserable sinners.

O GOD the holi ghost pceding from the father &c

O holy, blessed, and glorious Trinitie, thre persones and one God, haue merice, vpon vs miserable sinners

O holy blessed and glorious trinitie &.

Remembre not Lord, our offences nor the offeces of our forfathers, neither take thou vēgaūce of our sinnes

B.ij.   spare

spare vs good lorde, spare thy people, whom thou hast redemed wyth thy moste precious bloud, and bee not angry with vs for euer.

Spare vs good lord.

From all euil and mischiefe, from sinne, fro the craftis and assaultes of the deuil, from thy wrathe, and from euerlastyng dampnacion.

Good lord deliuer vs.

From blindnes of hart, from pride vain glory, and Hipocrisy, from enuie hatred, and malice, and all vncharytablenesse.

Good lorde deliuer vs.

From fornicacion, and al deadly sin and fro all the deceiptes of the world the fleshe and the deuell.

Good lord deliuer vs.

From lightening and tepest, from plague, pestilence & famine, from battaill & murdre, & from sodain death:

Good lord deliuer vs

From al sedicion and priute conspiracie, from the tiranny of the ▬▬▬▬
of

of Rome and all his detestable enormities, from all false doctryne and heresy, from all hardnes of hart and contempt of thy worde and commaundemente:

Good lorde deliuer vs

By the mistery of thy holy incarnacion, by thy holy natiutie and circumcision, by thy Baptisme, fasting, and temptacion.

Good lorde deliuer vs.

By thyne agony & bluddy sweate, by thy crosse and passion, by thy precious deth and buryall, by thy glorious resurreccyon and asscencion, by the commyng of the holy ghoste.

Good lorde deliuer vs.

In all tyme of our tribulacion, in al tyme of oure wealthe, in the houre of death, in the daie of Judgement

Good lorde deliuer vs.

we sinners do besech the to heare vs, O Lorde GOD, & that it may please thee to rule and gouerne thy holy Church vniuersall in the right waie.

We beseche the to heare vs good lorde.

That it may please the to kepe Edwarde the sixt, thy seruaunt, our king and gouernoure.

We &c

That it may please thee to rule his hearte in thi faith, feare and loue that he may alway haue affiaunce in the, and euer seke thy honour and glory.

We &c

That it maye please the too be his defendor and keper, geuing hym the victory ouer all his enemies.

We &c.

That it may please thee to illuminate al bishoppes, pastors, and ministers of the churche, with true knowledge and vnderstãding of thy worde and that bothe by theire preachyng and liuyng thei maie set it furthe and shewe it acordingly.

We &c

That it may please thee too endue the lordes of the counsall, and all the nobilitie with grace, wisedome, and
vnder

vnderstanding :

We &c

That it may please thee to blesse & kepe the magistrates. geuing them grace to execute iustice, and to maintein truthe :

We &c

That it may please thee to blesse and kepe all thy people :

We &c

That it may please thee to geue all nacions vnitie, peace and concorde :

We &c

That it may please the to geue vs an hearte to loue and dread thee, and diligently to lyue after thy comaundementes :

We &c

That it may please the to geue all thy people increase of grace, to heare mekely thy worde & to receue it with pure affecciō, and to bring fourth the fruictes of thy spirite :

We &c

That it may please the to brig into

to the waie of truth all suche as haue
erred and are deceyued.

We &c.

That it maie please thee to strengthe such as do stande, and to comfort
& help the weake harted, and to raise
vp them that fal, and finally to beate
doune Sathan vnder our feete.

We be &c

That it maie please the to succour,
helpe and comfort al that be in daunger, necessitie and tribulacion.

We &c.

That it maie please the to preserue
al that trauail by lande or by water,
all women laboryng with childe, all
sycke persones and young childzen, &
to shewe thy pitie vpon all prisoners
and captiues.

We &c

That it maie please the to defende
and prouide for the fatherlesse childre
and widowes, and all that bee deso-
late and oppressed.

We &c

That it may please the to haue mer
cie

cie vpon all men.

We beseche the to heare vs good Lorde.

That it may please thee to forgeue our enemies, persecutours and slaunderers, and to turne their hartes.

We beseche the to heare vs good Lorde.

That it may please the to geue and preserue to our vse the kyndely fruytes of the yearth so as in due tyme wee may inioye them.

We beseche the to heare vs good Lorde.

That it may please thee to geue to vs true repentaunce, to forgeue vs all our sinnes, negligences and ignoraunces, and to indue vs with the grace of thy holy spirite, to amende our lyues accordyng to thy holy worde.

We beseche the to heare vs good Lorde.

Sonne of God : we beseche thee to heare vs.

Sonne of God: we beseche the to heare vs.

O lambe of God, that takest away the synnes of the worlde.

Graunt vs thy peace.

O lambe of God, that takest awaie the synnes of the worlde.

L.i.   Haue

Haue mercie vpon vs.

O Christ heare vs.

O Christ heare vs.

Lorde haue mercie vpon vs.

Lorde haue mercie vpon vs.

Christ haue mercie vpon vs.

Christ haue mercie vpon vs.

Lorde haue mercie vpon vs.

Lorde haue mercie vpon vs.

Our father whiche art in heauen.

With the residue of the pater noster.

And leade vs not into temptacion.

But delyuer vs from euill. Amen.

The versicle.

O lorde deale not with vs after our synnes.

The aunswere

Neither reward vs after our iniquities.

Let vs praye.

God, mercifull father, that despisest not the syghyng of a contrite hart, nor the desire of suche as be sorowful, mercyfully assist our praiers, that we make before thee in all our troubles and aduersities, whensoeuer they oppresse vs. And graciously heare vs, that

that those euyls whiche the crafte and subtiltie of the deuill or man worketh against vs be brought to naught, and by the prouidence of thy goodnes, they maie bee dyspersed, that wee thy seruauntes, beyng hurt by no persecucions, maie euermore geue thankes vnto the, in thy holy church, through Jesu Christ our Lorde.

O Lorde, aryse, helpe vs and deliuer vs for thy names sake.

O God, we haue heard with our cares, and oure fathers haue declared vnto vs the noble workes that thou diddest in their daies, and in the olde tyme before them.

O lord, arise, help vs, & deliuer vs for thy honour.

Glory be to the father, & to the sonne and to the holy ghost: as it hath been from the beginning, is, & shalbee euer worlde without end. Amen.

Frō our enemies defend vs o Christ

Graciously loke vpon our afflicciōs.

Pitifully behold ȳ dolor of our hart.

Mercyfully forgeue the synnes of thy people.

Fauourably with mercie heare our

praiers.

O sonne of Dauid haue mercie vpon vs.

Bothe now and euer vouchesafe to heare vs Christ.

Graciously heare vs O Christ.

Graciously heare vs O Lorde Christ.

The versicle.

O Lorde, let thy mercie bee shewed vpon vs.

The aunswere

As we do put our trust in the.

Let vs pray.

WE humbly beseche thee, O father, mercyfully to loke vpon our infirmities, and for the glorie of thy name sake, turne from vs all those euilles, that we moste ryghteously haue deserued, and graunt that in all oure troubles, we may put all our whole trust & confidéce in thy mercy and euermore serue the in purenes of liuing to thy honour and glory, through our only mediatour and aduocate Iesus Christ our Lorde, Amen.

Almigh=

Almyghtie GOD, whiche haste geuen vs grace at this tyme with one accord to make our commune supplicacions vnto the, and doest promyse that whē two or thre be gathered together in thy name, thou wilt graunte their requestes: fulfyll now, O lorde, the desires and peticions of thy seruauntes, as may be moste expedient for theim, grauntyng vs in this worlde knowlege of thy truthe and in the worlde to come lyfe euerlastyng. Amen.

The Dirige.

Dilexi quoniam exaudiet. Psal. cxiiii.

℞ The laude and praise of God, through whose benefite we be preserued
in aduersitie.

I haue loued, for the lorde wil heare the voice of my praier.

For he hath inclined his eare vnto me, and in

my daies I wyll call vpon hym.

The sorowe of death hath compassed me, and the perilles of hel haue entangled me.

I haue found much trouble and sorowe, and I haue called vpon the name of the lord.

O lorde deliuer my soule, mercyfull lord and iust, our God is mercifull.

The Lorde preserueth the symple, I was brought lowe, and he delyuered me.

Turne into thy rest, O my soule, for the lord hath done muche for the.

For he hath deliuered my soule frō death, myne iyes from teares, my fete from slydyng.

I shall please the lorde, in the lande of the lyuyng.

Beatus qui intelligit. Psalm. xl.

℣ Happy is he that hath compassion vpon the poore, whom God deliuereth from his enemies, and preserueth euerlastingly.

Lessed is he that considereth the nedie and the poore: in the euyll day the Lord shall delyu=

deliuer him.

The lorde preserue him & kepe him alyue, and make hym fortunate in the yearth, and deliuer hym not into the wyll of his enemies.

The lord succour him being diseased in his bed, all his bed thou hast chaunged in his infirmitie.

I saied, Lorde haue mercy on me, heale my soule, for I haue trespassed against the.

Myne enemies spake euil vnto me, sayng, When shall he die, and his name perysshe?

And though he came in for to se, he spake vanities, his hart gathered mischiefe within hymselfe.

He went furth, & spake to the same purpose together.

Agaynst me dyd all myne enemies whisper, agaynst me haue they imagined me mischief.

They haue deuised an vntrue saiyng by me, shall he that slepeth haue no healpe to ryse agayn.

For the man with whom I was in peace, in whom I trusted, which hath eaten of my bread, made great meanes to supplant me.

But thou lord, haue mercy on me, and restore me, & I shall requite them.

By this I knowe thou fauourest me that myne enemy shall not triumphe vpon me.

But for mine innocencie thou hast defended me, and hast made me sure in thy syght for euer.

Blessed be the lorde God of Israell, world without ende, be it. be it.

Lauda anima mea dominum. Psalm. cxlv.

An exhortacion to praise God, and to put out trust in him, and not in me.

Rayse the Lorde, O my soule, I shall prayse the lorde duryng my lyfe, I shall syng prayse to my God as long as I lyue.

Put not their trust in princes, nor in the children of men, in whom there is no health.

His

His spirite shall passe out, and shal returne into his countrie, in that day shall all his thoughtes perishe.

Blessed is he whose helper is thee God of Jacob, whose hope is in his Lorde God, whiche make heauen and yearth and sea, and al that be in them.

Which kepeth truth euermore, doth iudgement to them that suffre wrong, and geueth meate to the hungery.

The lord lenseth them that be fettered, the lord geueth syght to the blynd.

The lorde lyfteth vp them that bee fallen, the lorde loueth the ryghteous.

The lord preserueth straungers, he wil defende the fatherles and wydow and wyll destroy the way of synners.

The Lorde thy God of Syon, shall reigne euermore from one generacion to another.

LOrde geue thy people eternall rest.

And lyght perpetuall shyne on them.

From the gates of hell.

Lord delyuer their soules.

M.i.   I

I truſt to ſe the goodnes of the lord.

In the lande of lyfe.

Lord heare my praier.

And let my crie come to the.

Let vs pray.

OOd to whom it is appropried to be merciful euer, and to ſpare, be mercyfull to the ſoules of thy ſeruãtes of eche kynd, and forgeue them all their ſinnes, that they being lenſed frõ the bondes of death, may aſcende vnto the lyfe euerlaſtyng : Through Chriſt our lorde. Amen.

O GOD the Lorde of pardone, graunt vnto the ſoule of N. thy ſeruaunte (the yeres mynde of whoſe death, we haue in remembraunce) a place of reſt, the bleſſull quiet and clerenes of thy lyght : Through Chriſte our lorde.

O God that art creatour and redemer of al faithful people : graũt vnto thee ſoules of all true beleuers being dead, remiſſion of all their ſynnes, that through deuout praiers thei

may

may obtayne thy gracious pardone,
that they haue alway desyred, whiche
shalt come to iudge the quicke and the
dead, and the worlde by fyre.

God haue mercy on all christen sou=
les. Amen.

Verba mea auribus. Psalm. v.

The godly persone desireth to be defended of
God, that the intentes of his aduersaries may
be stopped, and that the goodnes of God
may be shewed among the godly.

ORD, geue care vnto my wor=
des, vnderstād my clamour.

Herken vnto the voyce of
my praier, my king & my god

For vnto the will I praie, O lorde,
early shalt thou heare my voice.

Early shall I stand by the, and I
shall se that thou art a God that hath
no pleasure in iniquitie.

For the malicious shall not dwell
nere the, neither shal the vnrighteous
abyde before thyne iyes.

Thou hatest all that doo iniquitie,
thou shalt destroy al them that speake
lyes.

The lord doth abhorre the man that is bluddy and deceitfull.

But I through the plenteousnes of thy mercy shall enter into the house.

I wyll worship towardes thy holy temple in thy feare.

Leade me lorde into thy righteousnesse, because of myne enemies, direct my way in thy syght.

For in the mouth of them ther is no truthe, the hart of thē is ful of vanitie.

The throte of thē is an open graue disceytfully dyd they with their tounges, iudge them, O God.

Let them fall from their imaginacions, according to the greatnesse of their wyckednesse expel them, for they haue stirred the to anger, O lord.

And let all retoyce that trust in the, they shall euermore be glad, and thou shalt dwell among them.

And they shall glory in the, all that loue thy name, for thou wilt blesse the righteous.

Lorde thou hast crouned vs, as it were

were with a shilde of thy good wyll.

Dominus illuminatio mea. Psalm. xxvij

℣ The goodnesse of God toward his people.
wherby they be incoyraged to trust in God,
notwithstanding their aduersaries, to re=
ioyce in his ayde, and to magnifie him.

He Lorde is my light,
and my helth, whome
shall I feare:
The lorde is the de=
fendour of my lyfe, of
whō shal I be afraid:

Whiles the malicious approche vn=
to me for to deuoure my fleash.

Myne enemies whiche trouble me,
they were made weke, and fel doune.

If they pitche pauilions against me,
my hart shall not feare.

If a battaile rise agaynst me, I shal
trust in it.

One thing haue I asked of the lord
whiche I shall require, that I may in=
habit in the house of the Lorde all the
daies of my lyfe.

That I may see the beautie of the

M. iii. Lorde

Lord and may vysyte his temple.

For he hathe hyd me in his tabernacle in the euyll day, he hath defended me in the secrete place of his tabernacle.

He hath exalted me vpon a rocke,
and now he hath exalted myne hed a-
boue mine enemies that be about me.

And I haue offered in his tabernacle the sacrifice of laude, I shall syng
and say a psalme vnto the lord.

Heare my voyce lorde, wherwith I
haue cried vnto the, haue mercy on me,
and heare me.

Myne hart hath sayed vnto the, my
face hath sought the, lorde I shal seke
thy face.

Turne not thy face fro me, doo not
swarue fro thy seruaunt in anger.

Be mine helper, forsake me not, neither despyse thou me, O God my sauiour.

For my father & my mother, haue
forsaken me, but the Lorde hath taken me.

Lord

Lord teache me thy way, and leade me in a streight path, because of mine enemies.

Deliuer me not to the myndes of them that trouble me, for vniust witnesses haue rysen agaynst me, and haue spoken wickedly.

I trust to se the goodnes of God, in the lande of the lyuyng.

Abyde the lorde, doo manfully, and let thy hart be strengthed, and abyde the Lorde.

Quemadmodum desiderat. Psalm. xlí.

¶ The godly man is vexed with them that blaspheme Gods religion, and being pensife with feruent complaynt openeth his hart to God.

Uen as the hart longeth after the fontanes of waters, so doeth my soule long after the O God.

My soule hath thirsted after god the strong and lyuyng God, when shall I come & appere before the face of God.

My tearrs were to me day and night in

in steade of bread.

Whyleſt it is dayly ſaied vnto me, where is thy God?

Theſe thynges I haue called to mind and I haue powred furth my ſoule vnto my ſelfe, becauſe I ſhall departe into a place of maruelous habitacion vnto the houſe of God.

With a voice of gladnes and reioyſyng lyke the ſound of one that banketteth.

My ſoule, why art thou ſorowfull: and why doeſt thou trouble me.

Truſt in God, for I ſhall euer confeſſe him which is the helth of my coũtenaunce, and my God.

My ſoule within my ſelfe is troubled, therfore I ſhal haue the in mind, in the lande of Iordane, and the lytle mountayne of Hermon.

Depenes calleth vpõ depenes, with the noyſe of thy water conduſes.

Al thy raines and thy ſloudes haue runne ouer me.

In the day, the lord hath commaunded

ded his mercy, and in night his song is with me.

Prayer to the God of my life: I shal say vnto god, thou art my defendor.

Why hast thou forgotten, and why do I go all sorowfull, whyleste myne enemye doth afflicte me.

Whilest my bones are broken, myne enemies that haue troubled me, haue cast it in my teeth.

Whyleste they say to me euery day, where is thy god?

My solle whi art thou sorowful, and why doest thou trouble me.

Trust in God, for I shal euer confesse him, whiche is the health of my countenaunce, and my god.

The antheme

I Trust to se the goodnesse of the Lord in the land of the liuyng.

Lord graunt thy people euerlastyng reste.

And let thy euerlasting lyght shyne on theim.

Our father. &c.

R. j. And

And suffer vs not to be led into temptacion.

But deliuer vs from euill.

The .i. lesson

Thine hādes hath made me & fashioned me al together roūd about, & wilt thou destroy me lodeynly. O remembre that thou madest me as moulde of the yearth, and shalt bryng me into dust agayne. hast thou not put me together, as it were mylke, and hardened me to cruddes like cheese. Thou hast couered me with skinne and fleashe, and ioyned me together with bones and sinowes Thou hast graunted me lyfe and mercye and the diligent hede that thou takest on me, hath preserued my spirit.

The anthēme

I knowe that my redemer liueth & that I, the last day shal rise frō the yearth, and shal be cladde agayne with myne awne skinne, and in myne awne fleashe I shall se god, whom I my selfe shall se, and myne eyes

eyes shall loke vpon, and none other
this hope is layed vp in my bosome.

The seconde lesson.

Verely verily I saye vnto you. Iho. v.
He that heareth my word, & be=
leuith on him that sent me, hath
euerlasting life, and cōmeth not into
dampnacion, but passeth from death
to lyfe. Uerely verily I say vnto you,
the houre shall come, and nowe it is
when the dead shal heare the voyce of
the son of God, & they that heare shal
lyue: for as the father hath lyfe in hi
selfe, so likewise hath he geuen to the
sonne, to haue lyfe in him selfe, and
hath geuen hym power also to iudge,
bycause he is the sonne of man. Wer
uaile not at this for the houre cometh
in the which al that are in the graues
shall heare the voyce of the sonne of
god. And they that haue done good
shall come furth vnto the resurrectiō
of life, and they that haue done euyl,
vnto the resurrection of dampnatio n.

The antheme

N. H.   Bre=

Brethren, we wold not that ye sho=
ulde be ignoraunt as cõcerning
them the whych are fallẽ a sle pe
that ye sorow not as other do, which
haue no hope . For yf we beleue that
Iesus dyed and rose agayn : euen so,
them which slepe with Iesus, God
shall bring with him .

The iii lesson

Behold I shew you a mistery soth=
ly we shall all rise , but we shall
not all be chaunged . In a mom=
ment, in the twynklyng of an eye, at
the last trumpe , for the trumpe shall
blow, and the dead shall ryse incor=
ruptible, and we shalbe chaunged, for
this corruptible must put on icorrup=
tion, and this mortal must put on im
mortalitie, whẽ this corruptible hath
put on incorruption , and this mortal
hath put on immortalitie , then shall
be brought to passe the saying that is
writen:death is swalowed vp in vic=
tory, death where is thy victory? O
death where is thy sting? The stinge
of

of death is sinne, and the strength of
sinne is the lawe. But thankes be vn=
to God, which hath geuen vs victory,
thorowgh our Lord Jesus Christ.

The anthem.

Eliuer me good lord from eter=
nall death, in that dredful day
whē that heauē and yerth shal
be moued, & thou shalt iudge the worl
de byfire: This day is the dai of ire of
wretchednes and misery, the greate
day and very bitter.

Delyuer not to beastes, O lord, the
soules of them that confesse the, and
forget not at length the soules of thy
poore people.

Exaltabo te domine Psal. xxix.
Thankes be geuen for health recouered. The
goodnesse of god is praised who for a litle
aduersitie sendeth much comfort.

Wil exalte the O lorde, for
thou hast defended me and
not suffred mine enemies to
haue their pleasure vpō me.

O

O lorde my God I haue cried vnto thc, and thou hast healed me.

Lord thou hast brought my soll out of hell; thou haste perserued me from them that descend into the pyt.

Syng vnto the lorde, ye that be his sainctes, and geue thankes with a remembraunce of his holines.

For there is wrath in his displesure, and lyfe in his will.

At the euenings, waitinge shall abyde, but in the mornyng gladnesse.

In my welthynesse I layd, I shal neuer thou be remoued.

Lorde, through thy good wil thou gauest strength to my beautie.

Thou diddest turne thy face from me, and I was astonied.

Unto the, O lorde, wil I cry, and I will pray to my God.

What profyt is there in my bludd when I shal descend into corruption?

Shall dust geue thankes to the: or shall it declare thy truth?

The lord hath heard, an dhath ta-

keu

ken mercy on me, the lorde is made myne helper.

Thou haste turned my sorowe into ioy, thou haste cut of my sacke clothe, and hast compassed me with gladnes

That my glory myghte singe to the without griefe, O my Lorde God I shall euermore geue thankes to the.

Ego dixi. Psal. Esaie xxxviii.

Thankes for recouery of health

I Sayde, in the myddeste of my dayes, I shall go to the gates of hell.

I desyred the residue of my yeres I sayd, I shall not see the lord God, in the land of the lyuynge.

I shall se man no more, nor hym that dwelleth in rest.

My tyme is taken from me, and folden vp, as the Shepherdes tent.

My life is cut of, lyke a weauers webbe: when I yet beganne, he cutt me doune, from morninge, vntil the nyght thou wilt make an ende of me

I was, in hope vntil morninge but

as

as a Lyon, so he bꝛused al my bones:

From moꝛning vntil nighte , thou wilt make an ende of me as a younge swalowe so shal I chattre , and shal mourne as a doue .

Mine eyen daseled with lokyng on high .

Loꝛd I suffre foꝛce, answere foꝛ me what shal I say ꞏ oꝛ what shal he answeꝛe me, syns I haue done it ꞏ I shall remembꝛe all my yeres vnto the , with bitternesse of my harte.

Loꝛd yf lyfe be thus, and the lyfe of my spiric be after such soꝛt, thou shalt coꝛrect me, and quicke me: lo in peace my soꝛow is most bitter .

But thou haste deliuered my soule that it shoulde not perishe , thou hast cast behinde thy backe all my synnes.

Foꝛ neither hel shal knowledge the noꝛ deathe shall prayse the : they that descende into the pit, shal not loke foꝛ thy veritie .

He that is liuing, the lyuing person shal knowledge the like as I do now

the

the father to the chyldren shal declare thy truthe.

Preserue me O Lord, and wee shal sing our psalmes in the lordes house, all the daies of our lyfe.

In te domine speraui, Psalm. lxx.

C with God is our onely refuge, we must praie to hym, and in hym put all our truste, and hym prayse and magnifie.

In the (O Lord) haue I put my trust, let me neuer be confounded, in thy ryghteousnes deliuer me.

Inclyne thine eare vnto me, & make spede to saue me.

Be vnto me a protectour as God, & as a place offortresse for too saue me, for thou art my strength and refuge.

Deliuer me O my God, out of the hande of the synner, out of the hande of the lawe breaker, and the vniust.

For thou, O Lord, art my pacience, thou O Lorde arte my hope, euen fro my youth.

Through the haue I ben holden vp euer syns I was borne, thou arte my

defendour syns I came furthe of my
mothers wombe.

My synging alway is of the, I am
made as a wonder vnto manye, but
thou art a strong helper.

Let my mouthe be fylled wyth thy
praise, that I may synge thy glory and
thy magnificence all the day long.

Caste me not away in the tyme of age
forsake me not, when my strength fay-
leth me.

For myne enemies spake agaynste
me, and they that layde wayte for my
soule, dyd take their counsail together.

Saiyng, God hath forsaken hym, persecute hym, and take hym, for there is
none to deliuer hym.

Go not farre from me, O my God:
haue regarde to helpe me.

Let them be confounded and perish,
that are against my soule.

Let thē be couered with shame and
dishonour, that seke to do me euil.

But I wil alway trust, and I wyll
prase the more and more.

My mouth shall speake of thy righteousnes and thy saluacion al the day.

Because I knowe no letter, I wil entre into the strengthe of the Lorde: lorde I wyll make mencion of thy onely righteousnesse.

Thou o God, hast taught me from my youth hitherto, and I shall tell of thy wonderous workes.

And vnto age and oldenes, O God forsake me not.

Untill I shewe thy strengthe vnto generacions yet for to come.

Thy power, and thy righteousnes O God, vntyll the hyghest marueyle, Whiche thou haste wrought, O God, who is lyke vnto the:

O what greate & euyll aduersities hast thou shewed me: and yet diddest thou tprne and refreshe me: yea, and broughtest me again from the depnes of the yearth.

Thou hast multiplied vpon me thy magnificence, and thou hast returned and confoited me.

Therfore will I prayse the and thy

truth O God, in the instrumentes of musike, vnto the will I syng vpon the harpe whiche arte the holy GOD of Israell.

My lippes wilbe faine when I sing vnto the, and so wyll my soule alsoo, whiche thou hast redemed.

My togue also shal talke of thy righteousnesse al the day long, for they are confounded and brought vnto shame that seke to do me euill.

The antheme.

I Am the resurreccion & lyfe, he that beleueth in me, yea, although he were dead, yet shall he lyue, and who soeuer liueth and beleueth in me, shal not se euerlasting death.

Lorde haue mercy on vs.

Christ haue mercy on vs.

Our father whiche art in heauen. &c

And leade vs not into temptacion.

But deliuer vs from euill.

Lorde geue thy people eternal rest,

And lyght perpetuall shyne on them.

From the gates of hell.

Lorde

Lorde deliuer their soules.

I trust to se the goodnesse of the lorde.

In the lande of lyfe.

Lorde heare my praier.

And let my crie come to the.

Let vs praie.

O GOD, whiche by the mouthe of sainct Paule thyne Apostle hast taught vs, not to waile for them that slepe in Christ: graunt we beseche the that in the comming of thy sonne our Lorde Jesu Christe, both we and all other faithfull people beyng departed maye be graciously brought vnto the ioyes euerlasting, whiche shalt come to iudge the quicke and dead, and the world by fier. Amen.

ALmighty eternall God, to whom there is neuer any prayer made without hope of mercy, be mercifull to the soules of thy seruauntes being departed from this world in the confession of thy name, that they may be associat to the company of thy sainctes, through Christ our lord. Amen.

D. iij.   Lord.

LOrd, bowe thine eare vnto our prayers, wherein we deuoutly call vpon thy mercy, that thou wylt bestowe the soules of thy seruauntes (whiche thou hast commaunded to departe from this worlde) in the countrey of peace & rest, and cause them to be made parteners with thy holy seruauntes, through Christ our Lorde. Amen.

WE beseche the lord, that the praier of thy suppliauntes may auaile to the soules of thy seruãtes, that thou wilt both purge them of al their synnes, and cause them to be partakers of thy redempcion, whiche lyuest and reignest God, world without end. Amen.

God haue mercy on all christen soules.

(∴)

The comendaciõs.

This Psalmes is the A.B.C. of godly loue, the paradise of learning, the shoppe of the holy Ghost, the schole of the truthe: In whiche appereth howe the sainctes of God esteme his holy lawes, how feruently they be geuen vnto them, how it greueth them that they should be despised how feruently they desyre to learne them, to walke in them, and to fulfyl them: finally, howe the transgressours and aduersaries of them shalbe punished and destroyed.

(∴)

Blessed are they that be vnspotted in the way, whiche walke in the law of the lord Blessed are they that searche his testimonies, that seke him with all their hart.

For they that woorke wyckednes, haue not walked in his waies.

Thou hast commaunded thy commaundementes very streightly to bee kepte.

Wolde God my wayes myght bee directed to kepe thy iustificacions.

marginal note: Beati immaculati, psal. cxviii.

Then shall I not bee confounded, when I shal behold all thy commaundementes.

I shal confesse vnto the with a right hart, when I haue learned the iudgementes of thy righteousnes.

I shal kepe thy iustificacions, forsake me not vtterly.

Wherin doeth the young man correct his lyfe: in keping of thy wordes.

In quo corrige,&c.

With al my hart I haue sought the out, put me not away from thy commaundementes.

In my hart I haue hid thy wordes, that I might not offende the.

O lorde thou art blessed, teache me thy iustificacions.

With my lippes I haue bene telling all the iudgementes of thy mouth.

I haue had delight in the way of thy testimonies, as in all maner of riches.

I wylbe exercised in thy commaundementes, & I wyl consider thy wayes.

I wyl study in thy iustificacions, I

mull

wyll not forget thy wordes.

REward thy seruaunte, quicken me, and I shal kepe thy wordes

Retribue seruo. &c.

Open mine iyes, and I shal consider the marueilous thinges of thy lawe.

Retribue seruo &

I am a strauger in the land, hide not from me thy commaundementes.

My soule hath coueted to desyre thy iustificacions at all tymes.

Thou hast rebuked the proude, cursed are they whiche decline from thy commaundementes.

Take from me rebuke and contempt, for I haue sought after thy commaundementes.

For Princes haue ben set againste me, and thei spake against me, but thy seruaunt was still exercised in thy iustificacions.

For thy testimonies are my medita-cion, thy iustificacions are my counsail.

Adhesit a-umento a-nima.

My soule hath cleaued to y groud, quicke me accordig to thy word

I haue shewed thy waies, and thou hast heard me, teache me thy iustifica-tions.

B. i.

Tre

Instruct me in the way of thy iustificacions, and I shalbe exercised in
thy maruellous workes.

My soule hath slept for werynesse,
confirme me in thy wordes.

Remoue from me the way of iniquitie, and accordyng to thy lawe, haue
mercy on me.

I haue chosen the way of truthe, I
haue not forgotten thy nidgementes.

I haue cleaued to thy testimonies,
O lorde, put me not to confusion.

I haue runne the waye of thy com-
maundemetes, when thou hast enlarged myne hart.

Lege pone O Lorde, set the way of thy iustificacions to me for a lawe, and I
wyll euer seke it out.

Geue vnto me vnderstandyng, and
I shall searche thy law, and shal kepe
it with myne whole hart.

Leade me in the path of thy commaundementes, for that I haue desyred.

Bowe myne hart into thy testimonies, and not into coueteousnesse.

Turne

Turne away myne iyes, that they
se not vanitie, quicken me in the way.

Set thy worde vnto thy seruaunt in
thy feare.

Cut of my rebuke, that I am afraid
of, for thy iudgementes be good.

Lo, I haue desyred thy commaundementes: & in thine equitie quicken me

And let thy mercy come vpon me
O lorde, and thy healthe accordyng to thy promise.

Et veniat su
per me mi-
sericordia
tua,

And I shall aunswere to them that
vpbrayd me, for I haue trusted in thy
wordes.

And take not the woorde of truthe
from my mouthe vtterlye, for I haue
muche trusted in thy iudgementes.

And I will kepe thy lawe alwaye,
world without ende.

And I haue walked at large, for I
haue sought thy commaundementes.

And I spake of thy testimonies in
the syght of kynges, and I was not
ashamed.

And I haue mused on thy commaun

P. ij.   demen-

dementes whiche J haue loued.

And J haue lift vp mynt handes to thy commaundementes, whiche J haue loued, and J shalbe occupied in thy iustificacions.

Remember thy worde to thy seruaunt, in whiche thou hast geuē me hope.

The same hath cōforted me in mine affliction, for thy worde hath quickened me.

The proude men haue doen wickednesse on euery syde, but J haue not swarued from thy lawe.

J haue bene myntfull of thy iudgementes good lord, from the beginning of the worlde, and haue bene cōforted.

J haue fayted, because of synners that forsake thy lawe.

Thy iustificacions were my songes in the place of my wayfaryng.

In the night season J haue thought of thy name, O lorde, and J haue kept thy lawe.

J had this, because J searched out thy

thy iustificacions.

O Lorde, thou art my porcion, I haue promised to kepe thy lawe.

Porcio mea domine

I haue besought thy maiestie with all my harth, haue mercy on me accordyng to thy worde.

I haue considered my waies, and I haue turned my feete into thy testimonies.

I am redy, and I am not troubled to kepe thy commaundementes.

The bondes of sinners haue be wrapt me, and I haue not forgotten thy lawe.

I rose vp in the middes of the night to geue the thankes for the iudgementes of thy iustificacion.

I am partaker of al that feare the, and of them that kepe thy commaundementes.

O lord, the yearth is ful of thy mercy, teache me thy iustificacions.

T Hou hast delt gently with thy seruaunt O Lorde, accordyng to thy worde.

Bonitatem fecisti,

Teache me goodnesse, learnyng and

P. iij.   know:

knowlege, for I haue beleued thy cō=
maundementes.

Before I was humbled, I did sinne
therfore I haue kept thy worde.

Thou art good, and in thy goodnes
teache me thy iustificacions.

The iniquitie of proud men is mul=
tiplied vpon me, but I with all my
whole hart shall searche out thy com=
maundementes.

Their hart is congeled lyke mylke;
but I haue thought vpon thy comma=
undementes.

It is good for me that thou hast hū=
bled me that I may learne thy iustifi=
cacions.

The lawe of thy mouth is dearer to
me, then thousandes of golde or siluer.

Manus tue. Thy handes haue made me, and
fashioned me: geue me vnderstā=
ding to learne thy cōmaundementes.

They that feare the shall se me, and
be glad, because I haue trusted muche
in thy wordes.

I know O lord, that thy iudgemē=
tes

tes are right, and in thy truthe thou
hast humbled me.

Let thy mercy be to cõfort me accor
ding to thy worde, vnto thy seruaunt.

Let thy mercyes come to me, and I
shall lyue, for thy lawe is my study.

Let the proude whiche wrongfully
haue done wickednes vnto me, be confounded and I will be occupied in thy
commaundementes.

Let thẽ be turned to me which feare
the, ꝓ thei that know thy testymonies.

Let mine hart be immaculate in thy
iustificaciõs, that I be not cõfounded.

My soule hath longed for thy saluacion, ꝓ I haue trusted muche
vnto thy worde.

Mine iyes haue longed for thy promise, saiyng, whẽ wilt thou cõfort me?

For I am made lyke a bottell in the
smoke, I haue not forgotten thy iustificacions.

How many be the dayes of thy seruaunt, when wilt thou geue iudgemẽt
of them that persecute me?

Defecit in
salutare.

Wicked

Wicked men haue told me fables, but not after thy lawe.

All thy commaundemētes is truth, wicked men haue persecuted me, succour me.

They had almoste made an ende of me in the yearth, but I haue not forsaken thy commaundementes.

Quicken me according to thi mercy, and I shall kepe the testimonies of thy mouth.

In eternum domine. O Lorde, thy woorde endureth in heauen euerlastingly.

Thy truthe remaineth from generacion, thou hast founded the yearth, and it abydeth.

By thyne ordinaunce the daie continueth, for al thinges obey vnto the.

Except thy lawe had bene my meditacion, peraduenture I had perished in my trouble.

I shal neuer forget thy iustificaciōs for in them thou hast quickened me.

I am thine, saue me, for I haue sought out thy iustificacions.

Sinners

Synners haue wayted me too destroye me, I haue vnderstand thy testymonyes.

I se that all perfection hath an ende thy commaundement is very brode.

O Lord, how much haue I loued thy lawe, it is my studye all the day long. *Quomodo dilexi.*

Thou hast made me wise ouer mine enemies throughe thy commaundementes, for it is euer with me.

I haue perceiued more then al that taught me, for thy testimonies were my meditation.

I haue perceiued more then auncient men, bycause I haue searched thy commaundementes.

I haue kepte my feete from euery euyll waye, that I myghte kepe thy woordes.

I haue not declined frō thy iudgementes, for bicause thou hast set me a lawe.

Howe swete be thy woordes vnto my taste, & to my mouth sweter then hony.

M.i I

I haue taken vnderstanding of thy commaundementes, therfore haue I hated euery way of iniquitie.

Lucerna
pebidue
meis

Thy worde is a Lanterne vnto my feete, and a lighte vnto my pathes.

I haue sworne and decreed to kepe the iudgementes of thi righteousnes

O lord I am brought lowe on euerysyde, quicken me accordyng to thy worde.

The voluntarye offerynges of my mouth, make them acceptable, o lord, and teache me thy iudgementes.

My soule is euer in my handes, and I haue not forgotten thy lawe.

Synners haue set a snare for me, I haue not erred from thy commaundementes.

I haue gotten thi testimonies by inheritaunce for euer, for because thei be the ioy of myne hart.

Bowe mine hart to do thy iustifications euermore for rewarde.

I

I Haue hated the wicked, & haue Iniquos
I loued thy lawe.
odio habui

Thou art my helper & my defender
and I haue trusted much i thy word.

O ye wicked, bow fro me & I shal
serche the comaundemetes of my God.

Receiue me accordyng to thy word
and I shal liue, and confound me not
otherwise then I loke for

Help me & I shalbe safe and shalbe
occupied in thy iustificacions euer.

Thou hast dispised al that go from
thy iudgementes, for their thoughtes
were vniust.

I haue reputed all sinners of the
earth for offenders, therefore I haue
loued thy testimonies.

Strike my fleshe with thi feare, for
I am a frayde of thy iudgementes.

I Haue doone iustice and righte= Feci iudi
I ousnesse, delyuer me not to them cium
that falsly blame me

Receiue thi seruaunt into goodnes
let not proude men falsely blame me.

Myne eyes are wasted in lokyng for
Q.ij. thy

thy health, and ÿ word of thy iustyce.

Do to thi seruaūt according to thy merci and teach me thy iustifications

I am thy seruaūte, geue me vnderstandyng, that I may knowe thy testimonies.

It is tyme to do, O Lorde, for thei haue broken thy lawe.

Therfore I haue loued thy cōmaūdementes aboue gold and Topace

And therfore I was ledde to al thi commaundementes, I haue hated euery wicked waie.

Mirabilia testimonia

O lord meruilous be thy testimonies, therefore my folke hath searched theim.

The declaration of thy wordes dothe illumine and geue vnderstanding to the simple.

I opened my mouth and drue in my breathe, for I desyred thy comaundementes.

Loke vpon me and haue mercy vpō me accordyng to the iudgemēt of thē that loue thy name.

Direct

Direct my goinges according to thy word, & let no siquitie reigne ouer me.

Redeme me from the false blame of men, that I may kepe thy commaundementes,

Lighten thy face vpon thy seruaunt and teache me thy iustifications.

Myne eyes haue broughte furth stremes of water, bycause they haue not kept thy lawe.

Iustus es tu domine

Righteous art thou Lorde, and righteous is thy iudgemente.

Thou haste commaunded iustice in thy testimonies & truthe most chiefly.

My zeale hath caused me to consume bycause myne enemies forgat thye wordes.

Thi woorde is vtterlye tryed with fire, and thy seruaunt loued it.

I am yong & set at nought, yet haue I not forgotten thy commaundmentes.

Thy iustice is iustyce euerlastyng and thy lawe is truthe,

Trouble and heurnesse haue entangled me, thy commaundementes are my study.

Thy

Thy testimonies be equitie euerlastyngly, geue me vnderstandyng, and I shall lyue.

Clamaui
in toto cor
de meo

I Haue called with my whoole harte, heare me lord, for I shall searche thy iustifications.

I haue cryed vnto the, saue me that I may obserue thy comaundementes

I haue preuented in tyme, and haue cryed, for I haue greatlye trusted in thy woordes.

Myne eyes haue preuēted the dawnyng of the day, for to study thy woordes.

Lord heare my voyce accordyng to thy mercy, and quicken me accordyng to thy iudgement.

They that persecute me haue drawen nigh to wickednesse.

And from thy lawe they are gone farre wide.

Lord thou art nere at hand, and all thy wayes are very truthe.

At the beginnyng I had knowledge of thy testimonies, for thou hast established

blished them for euer.

BEholde my trouble and delyuer
me, bycause I haue not forgot=
ten thy lawe.

Vide hu=
militatem
meam,

Judge my cause & redeme me. quicke
me accordyng to thy worde.

Health is farre from synners for thei
haue not searched out thi iustificatiōs

Thy mercy Lord is muche accor=
dyng to thy righteousnes quicken me.

Many there be which persecute me
and trouble me, I haue not swarued
from thy testimonies.

I sawe the offendours & I was ast=
onied, because thei kept not thi word.

Behold Lord for I haue loued thy
commaundementes, quicke me in thy
mercy.

The beginnyng of thy word is ve=
ritie, al thy iudgementes are iustice e=
uerlastingly.

THe princes haue persecuted me
without cause, and my harte
hath bene a drad of thy worde.

Principes
persecuti
sunt

I shall be glad of thy wordes as he
that

that hath founde many spoyles.

I haue hated iniquitie, and haue abhorred it, but thy lawe I haue loued.

Seuē times in the day haue I praised the, because of thy righteous iudgementes.

Great peace is to them that loue thy lawe, and they are not offended.

I loked for thy saluacion, O lorde, & loued thy commaundementes.

My soule hath kept thy testimonies, and hath loued them greately.

I haue kept thy commaundemētes and thy testymonies, for all my waies are in thy syght.

O Lorde, lett my prayer approche nere in thi sight, geue me vnderstanding according to thy woorde.

Appropinquet depre catio.

O lorde, let my praier enter into thy syght, delyuer me accordyng to thy woorde.

My lyppes shall powre furthe thy prayse when thou haste taught me thy iustificacions.

My tong shal shew furth thy word,

for

for all thy commaundemētes are equitie.

Let thy hande be redy to helpe me, for because I haue chosen thy commaundementes.

O Lorde I haue desyred thy helth, and thy lawe is my study.

My soule shall liue and prayse the, & thy iudgementes shall helpe me.

I haue wādered like a sheye which was lost, O lord, seke out thy seruaūt, for I haue not forgotten thy commaundementes.

Deus deus meus. Psalm xxi.

The Psalmes of the Passion.

The discription of the passion of our sauiour Christ, and of his aduauncement and kyngdome.

GOD, my GOD, loke towarde me, why haue thou forsaken me, farre fro my health be the workes of my complaynt.

My God I crye and call to the by day, but thou hearest me not, and likewyse by night and cease not.

But thou dwellest in the holy place, O the worship of Israell, our fathers trusted in the: they trusted, and thou didest deliuer them.

They cried to thee, and they were made safe, they trusted in thee, and they were not confounded.

I truely am but a worme, and no man, the rebuke of men, and an outcast of all the people.

Al they that se me, laugh me to scorne, they spake with their lyppes, and nodded their heades.

Saiyng, he trusted in the Lord, now let him deliuer him, let hym saue hym for he loueth hym.

For thou art he that tokest me oute of my mothers wōbe, & wast my hope from my mothers brestes, to the I was cast out from my natiuitie.

Thou arte my God, from my mothers wombe, depart not from me.

For tribulacion is nere at hande, & there is none to helpe me.

Many calues haue compassed mee,
and

and fat bulles haue beset me about.

They haue set their mouthes wyde open vpon me lyke a Lyon rampyng and roryng.

I am poured furth lyke water, and all my bones be dispersed asunder.

My hart is made like melting waxe in the middes of my belly.

My strength is dried vp like a sherd my tonng cleaueth fast to my iawes and thou hast brought me into the dust of death.

For many dogges compassed me about, the counsaill of the wicked haue beset me.

They pearsed my handes & my fete, they haue numbred all my bones.

Thei stode staring and loking vpon me, they deuided my garmentes amōg thē, and vpon my cote they cast lottes.

But thou, O lorde, prolong not thy helpe from me, loke to my defence.

Deliuer my soule from the swerde, and myne only soule from the power of the dogge.

Saue me from the mouth of the Lion, and myne humilitie from the hornes of Unicornes.

I shal shew thy name to my brethre and I shal prayse the in the middes of the congregation.

Ye that feare the lord, prayse ye hym all the hole sede of Iacob glorifie hym

Let al the seede of Israel feare hym for he despised not, nor disdayned not the prayer of the poore.

Nor he turned not his face away frō me, and when I cryed vnto hym he hearde me.

The shal I prayse in the great congregatiō, I wil perfourme my vowes in the sight of them that feare hym.

Pore men shal eate, and shalbe satisfied, and thei shal prayse the lord that seke after him, their hartes shall liue worlde without ende.

Al the coastes of the yearth shal remembre thiem selfes, and shalbe conuerted to the Lorde.

And all nations of people shall doo wor=

worship in his sight.

For the kingdome is the lordes, and he shall rule the people.

Al such as be fatte vpon the yearth haue eaten & worshipped, all that shal descend into the yearth shal fal downe in his syght.

And my soule shal lyue to him, and my sede shall serue hym.

The generacio to come shalbe shewed to the Lorde, and the heauens shal shew his iustice to the people that shal be borne, whiche the lord hath made.

Saluum me fac deus, Psalm. lxix.

¶ The complaint of Christ and his churche of their great aduersities. A feruēt prater for deliueraunce. The aduersaries of God be cursed. An harty thankesgeuing for helpe obtained.

Aue me o God, for ye waters are entred vnto my soule.

I sticke fast in ye depe myre where no grounde is.

I am come into the depe of the sea, and the tēpest hath ouerwhelmed me.

R. iii.   I haue

I haue trauailed criyng, my throte is made hoarſe, my ſyghte hath fayled while I truſted in my God.

They that hate me without cauſe are mo then the heares of my head.

They that are myne enemies, and haue perſecuted me giltles, are mightie, I payed then the thynges that I neuer toke.

God, thou knoweſt my ſymplenes, and my fautes are not hyd from the.

Let not them that truſt in the, o lord god of hoſtes, be aſhamed for my cauſe

Let not thoſe that ſeke the, be confounded through me, O Lord God of Iſraell.

For I haue ſuffered reprofe for thy ſake, ſhame hath couered my face.

I am become a ſtraunger vnto my brethren, and an aliaunt vnto my mothers children.

For the zeale of thine houſe hath eaten me, and the rebukes of them that rebuked the, are fallē vpon me, I chaſtened my ſelfe with faſting, and that
was

was turned to my reprofe.

I put on an heere cole also, and they iested vpon me.

They that sat in the gate spake against me, and they that dranke wyne made songes vpon me.

But lorde, I make my prayer vnto the in the time of thy good wil, o God. Heare me in the multitude of thy mercies, in the trueth of thy saluacion.

Take me out of the myre, that I sticke not, deliuer me from them that hate me, and out of the depe waters.

Let not the tempest of water droune me, neither the depe swallow me vp, & let not the pit shut her mouth vpon me.

Heare me O Lord, for thy mercy is kynde, loke vpon me accordyng vnto the multytude of thy mercies.

And turne not thy face from thy seruaunt, for I am in trouble, heare me spedely.

Take hede to my soule & saue it, deliuer me because of mine enemies.

Thou knowest my reproue, my shame

me and my dishonour.

All they that trouble me are in thy syght, my hart hath loked for rebuke and wretchednes.

I looked for some to be heauy with me, and there was none too comfort me, and I found none.

They gaue me gal to eate, & when I was thirsty, they gaue me bitter drink

Let their table be made a snare to the & a rewarde, & an occasion of fallyng.

Let their eyes be blinded that they se not, & euer bow doune their backes.

Poure out thyne indignacion vpon them, and let thy wrathful displeasure take holde of them.

Let their habitacion be voyde, and no man dwell in their tentes.

For they haue persecuted hym who thou hast smitten, and they haue enccealed the payne of my woundes.

Ley vpon them wickednesse vpon wickednes, and let them not entre into thy ryghtcousnes.

Let them be wyped out of the boke
of

of the lyuyng, and let thē not be written with the iuſt.

I am poꝛe and ſoꝛowfull, thy health
O God, hath taken me vp.

I wyll pꝛaiſe the name of god with
a ſong, and magnify him with pꝛayſe.

And it ſhall pleaſe god, better then
a yong Bullocke that beareth hoꝛnes
and houes.

Let the pooꝛe conſider and be glad,
ſeke after God, & your ſoule ſhall lyue.

Foꝛ the Loꝛde hath heard the pooꝛe
and hath not diſpiſed his pꝛiſoners.

Heauen and yearth pꝛaiſe hym, the
ſea and all that crepeth in them.

Foꝛ God ſhal ſaue Sion, and the ci-
ties of Iuda ſhalbe builded, and they
ſhall dwel there, & they that inherit it.

The poſterite alſo of his ſeruauntes
ſhall poſſeſſe it, and they that loue hys
name ſhall dwell therin.

Deus deus ſalutis. Pſal. lxxxvij.

¶ A greuous complaint of the godly perſone ex-
tremely handled with diſeaſes and perſecu-
tions, and that without any conſole.

Ex. i.   ¶ Lord

O Lord God of my health, I haue cried daye and night before the.

Let my prayer entre into thy presence, bowe thine eare vnto my prayer.

For my soule is full of aduersities, and my life draweth nighe vnto hel.

I am counted as one of thẽ that go doune into the pit, and I am as a man without helpe, free among the dead.

Like vnto them that be wounded & lye in the graue, whome thou remembrest no more, and are put away from thy hande.

They haue laid me in the lower pit in darke places, and in the shadowe of death.

Thine indignacion is fast vpon me, and thou haste laied vpon me all thy waues.

Thou hast put away mine aquayntaunce farre from me, they take me as abhominable.

I am betraied, I cannot get furth:

my

my syght waxed dymme for lacke.

Lorde, I called vpon the the whole daye, vnto the haue I stretched oute mine handes.

Wilt thou shew wōders to the dead or shal the phisicions raise men again to prayse the?

Shall any man shewe thy mercy in the graue & thy truthe in destruccion?

Shall thy wonderous workes bee knowen in the darke, and thy ryghteousnes in the lande of forgetfulnes?

And I haue to the cried o lorde, and early shall my praier come before the.

Lord doest thou reiecte my soule, & turnest thou thy face from me?

I am pore & in trauailes euen from my youth, and whē I was exalted I was casten doune and troubled.

Thy wrath hath passed ouer me & thy terrours haue troubled me sore.

They came round about me all day lyke water, and cōpassed me togethcr

My louer and frend hast thou put awaye farre from me, & myne acquayn

taunce

teares for my wretchednes.

Quare fremuerunt gentes. Psal. ij.

¶ The rage of the people against Christ. Christ
is ordeined a kyng of his father. Rulers be
exhorted to godly knowlege.

Hy hath the Heathē raged:
¶ why hath the people imagined vayne thynges?

The kynges of the year-
the stode vp, and the rulers came together against the Lorde, and agaynst
his Christ.

Let vs breake their bondes asonder
and let vs cast awaye their yoke from
vs.

He that dwelleth in heauen shall
laugh them to scorne, and the lord shal
haue them in derision.

Then he will speake vnto theim in
his wrath, and vexe theim in his sore
displeasure.

I truly am made kyng of hym, ouer
Syon his holy hil, preaching his pre-
cept.

The Lorde sayd to me, thou art my
sonne, this daie haue I begotten the.

Also

Aske of me, and I shal geue the, the Gentyles for thyne inheritaunce, and the vtter part of the yearth for thy possession.

Thou shalt rule them with an yron rod, and breake theim in peces lyke a potters vessell.

And now ye kynges vnderstand, be learned ye that iudge the yearth.

Serue the lord in feare, and reioyce to him with reuerence.

Get discipline that the lorde bee not angry, & ye perish from the right way.

When his angre shalbe kyndled for a short whyle, blessed are all they that trust in hym.

Eripe me de inimicis. Psalm. lviii.

¶ The praier of Christ, for hymselfe and for his brethren, against his persecutours.

DEliuer me from myne enemies O my God, delyuer me from them that ryse against me.

Deliuer me from the workers of wikednes, saue me from the bludsheders.

For lo, they haue catched my soule,

S. iii.   For

stoute men haue assaulted me.

There is no iniquitie nor faute in me
o lord, without iniquitie haue I runne
and dyrected my way.

Arise to succour me and loke, & thou
lorde God of might, God of Israel.

Stirre to visite al the gentiles, haue
mercy of none that woorke iniquitie.

They shalbe conuerted at eue n, and
shalbe as hungry as dogges, and shal
compasse about the citie.
Lo, thei wil speake with their mouth
and a swerd is in their lippes, for who
hath heard:

And thou lorde shalt haue them in
derision, and thou shalt bring all gentiles to nought.

My strength I wil ascribe to the, for
thou art God my defendour, my God
his mercy will preuent me.

God sheweth me how I should deale
with mine enemies, kill theim not lest
my people might forget.

Scatter them abrode by thy mighte
& put the donne o lord my protectour.

For

For the sinne of their mouthe, & for the wordes of their lyppes, let them be taken in their pryde.

For their blasphemy and liyng, they shalbe notified to be destroyed.

In the wrath of destructio, and they shal not remayne, and thei shal know that God hathe rule ouer Iacob and ouer all the coastes of the worlde.

They shalbe conuerted at euen, and shalbe as hungry as dogges, and shall compasse about the citie.

Thei scat.er abrode for meat:, if thei haue not ynough, thei wil murmur.

As for me, I will sing of thy power. & praise thy mercy betime in the morʒnyng.

For thou hast bene my defendoure, and refuge, in the daye of my trouble.

Unto the, O my helper, will I syng for thou O God, arte my defendoure, my god, my mercy.

The

¶ The Passion of our sauiour Iesu Christ, written by saint Ihon

Esus wēt furth with his disciples ouer the broke Cedron, where was a gardē, into the which he entred with his disciples. Judas also (which betraied hym) knew the place, for Jesus often times resorted thither with his disciples. Judas then after that he had receiued a bond of men and ministers of the high priestes and Pharisies, came thither with lanternes and cressettes and wepons. Then Jesus knowing al thinges that should come on hym, went furth and sayd vnto them: whō seke ye? They answered hym, Jesus of Nazareth, Jesus saied vnto thē: I am he. Judas also which betraied hī stod with them. But assone as he had saied vnto them, I am he, they wente backwardes and fell to the grounde. And he asked them agayn, whō seke ye? Thei saiD, Jesus of Nazareth: Je=
sus

ſus anſwered, I ſaie vnto you, I am
he, if then ye ſeke me, let theſe go their
way, that the ſaiyng mighte be fulfilled which he ſpake: of thē which thou
gaueſt me, haue I not loſt one. Simō
Peter had a ſworde and dꝛewe it, and
ſmote the high pꝛieſtes ſeruaunt and
cut of his right eare: The ſeruaun=
tes name was Malcus. Then ſayed
Ieſus vnto Peter, put vp thy ſworde
into the ſheath, wylt thou not that I
ſhal dꝛink of the cup which my father
hath geuen me? Then the companye
and the captaine and the miniſters of
the Iewes toke Ieſus & bound hym
and led him awaye to Anna firſt, foꝛ
he was father in lawe vnto Caiphas
whiche was the high pꝛieſt the ſame
yere. Caiphas was he that gaue coū=
ſail to the Iewes, that it was expedi=
ent that one mā ſhould die foꝛ the peo
ple. And Symon Peter folowed Ieſus and another diſciple: the diſciple
was knowen of the high pꝛieſt, & wēt
in with Ieſus into the palace of the

T.ſ.   high

high priest, but Peter stode at the dore
without. Then wet out the other dis
ciple which was knowen vnto ẏ high
priest and spake to the damosell that
kept the dore, and broughte in Peter.
Then said the damosell that kept the
dore vnto Peter, arte not thou one of
this mans disciples to: He denied it, ẻ
said, I am not. The seruauntes and
the ministers stode there, ẻ had made
a fier of coles for it was cold, and thei
warmed them selues. Peter also stode
emong them and warmed hym selfe:
Then the high priest asked Iesus of
his disciples and of his doctrine. Ie=
sus answered him, I spake openly in
the world. I euer taught in the Sina.
goge and in the tẽple, whether all the
Iewes resort, ẻ in secret haue I sayd
nothing : why askest thou me: Aske
them which heard me what I said vn
to them. Behold, they can tel what I
sayd. whã he had thus spoken, one of
the ministers which stode by, smot Ie
sus on the face, saiyng answerest thou
the

the high prieſt ſo: Jeſus anſwered hi
if J haue euil ſpoke, bear witnes of e-
uil, if J haue wel ſpoken, why ſmyteſt
thou me: And Annas ſent him bouͦd
vnto Caiphas the highe prieſt. Simoͦ
Peter ſtode & warmed him ſelfe. And
they ſayd vnto hi, art not thou one of
his diſciples to: He denied it, and ſayd
J am not. One of the ſeruaūtes of the
high prieſt, his coſin, whoſe ear peter
ſmoteof, ſaied vnto him: Did not J ſe
the in the garden with him: Peter denied it agayn, & immediateli the cocke
crew. Then led they Jeſus from Caiphas into the hal of iudgemét, it was
in the mornyng, and thei theim ſelues
wét not into the iudgement hal, leaſt
thei ſhoulde bee defiled, but that they
might eate the Paſchal lambe. Pilat
then wét out vnto them & ſayd: what
accuſatioͦ bring you againſt this maͦ.
Thei anſwered and ſaid vnto him, if
he were not an euil doer we wold not.
haue delyuered hym vnto the. Then
ſaid Pilat vnto them. Take ye him, &

iudge him after your awne law. Thé
the Jewes sayed vnto him . It is not
lawful forvs to put any mã to death
that ý words of Jesus might be fulfilled, whiche he spake, signifiyng what
death he should dye. Then Pilat entred into the iudgement hall agayne,
and called Jesus, and sayd vnto hym
arte thou the kyng of Jewes: Jesus
answered, saist thou that of thy selfe,
or did other tel ý of me: Pilat answe=
red: Am J a Jewe: Thine owne nation and high priestes haue deliuered
the vnto me, what hast thou done: Je
sus answered: my kingdom is not of
this world, if my kingdõ were of this
world, then wold my ministers surely
fight, that J shoulde not be deliuered
to the Jewes, but nowe is my kyng=
dome not rom thence. Pylat sayd vnto him, Art thou a king then: Jesus ã·
swered, Thou saiest that J am a kig
for this cause was J borne, & for this
canse came J into the worlde, that J
should beare witnes vnto the truthe,
And

And all that are of the truth, here my voice. Pylat sayed vnto him, what is truth: And when he had said that, he went out againe vnto the Iewes, & sayd vnto thē, I fynd in him no cause at al, ye haue a custome that I should deliuer you one lose at Easter: will ye that I lose vnto you the kyng of the Iewes: Thē cried they al agayn sayyng, not him but Barrabas: that Barrabas was a robber. Thē Pilat toke Iesus and scourged him. And ƒ souldiers woſld a croune of thornes and put it on hys heade, and did on him a purple garment, and sayd: Haile king of the Iewes, and they smote him on the face. Pilat went furth again, and sayd vnto them. Behold I bring him furth again to you, that ye mai know that I finde no faulte in hym, Then came Iesus furth, wearyng a croune of thorne, & a roabe of purple : And Pylat sayd vnto thē, behold the man. whā the high priestes and ministers sawe him, they cried, saiyng, Crucifie

hym

him, crucifie him. Pilat ſaid vnto thē
Take ye hym and crucifie hym, foꝛ I
fynd no cauſe in him. The Jewes anſwered him, we haue a law, ⁊ by the
lawe he ough to dye, be cauſe he made
him ſelfe the ſonne of God. when Pilat hard that ſaiyng, he was the moꝛe
afraied, and went again into the iudgemēt hal, ⁊ ſaid vnto Jeſus: whence
art thou? But Jeſus gaue hym no an
ſwere. Thē ſaid Pilat vnto hi. Spae-
keſt thou not vnto me? knoweſt thou
not that I haue power to crucifie the
and haue power to deliuer the? Jeſus
anſwered: Thou couldeſt haue no po
wer at al againſt me, except it wer geuen the from aboue Therfoꝛ, he that
deliuered me vnto the hath the moꝛe
ſinne. And from thence forth ſoughte
Pilat meanes to deliuer him, but the
Jewes cryed, ſaiyng, if thou let hym
go, thou art not Ceaſars frend, foꝛ
whoſoeuer maketh him ſele a king is
againſt Ceſar. whā Pilat heard that
ſaiyng, he bꝛoughte Jeſus furth and
ſate

sate doune to geue sentence, in a place
called the Pauemēt, but in the Hebru
Gabbatha. It was Pasch euē, about
the sirt hour. And he saied vnto ẏ Ie=
wes. Behold your kyng: but thie cri=
ed away with him, awaye with hym,
Pilat said vnto them. Shal I crucifie
your kyng? The high priestes answe=
red, we haue no king but ceasar. Thē
deliuered he him vnto them to be ccu=
cified, And they toke Iesus ⁊ led him
away, and he bare his crosse, and wēt
furthe into a place called the place of
dead mens sculles (whiche is named
in Hebrue Golgatha) Wher thei cruci=
fyed hym. And wyth him. ij. other, on
ether side one, ⁊ Iesus in the middes.
Pylat wrote a title, and put it on the
crosse. The wrytyng was Iesus of
Nazareth kyng of the Iewes. This
title red manye of the Iewes, for the
place wher Iesus was crucified, was
nigh to the citie. And it was writtē in
Hebrue, Greke, and Latine. Thē said
the hyghe pryestes of the Iewes to
Pilate,

Pilat, wryte not kyng of Jewes, but that he said, J am king of the Jewes Pylat anſwered: what J haue writē that haue J wirtten. Thē the ſoldyers whē thei had crucified Jeſ⁹, toke hys garmentes and made foure partes. to eueri ſoulldier a part, ¶ alſo his coat. The coate was without ſeame wrought vpō throughout. And thei ſayd one to another, let vs not diuide it, but let vs caſt lotts, who ſhal haue it. That the ſcripture myght be fulfil led, whych ſaith: They parted my rai ment emong thē, and on my coat they caſt lottes. And the ſouldiers did this in deede. There ſtoode by the croſſe of Jeſus, hys mother and hys mothers ſiſter, Mari the wife of Cleophas, ¶ Mari Magdalen. whan Jeſus ſawe hys mother and the diſciple ſtanding whom he loued, he ſayd vnto his mother: woman, behold thy ſonne: Thē ſayde he to the diſciple: beholde thy mother, and from that houre the dyſ ciple toke her for hys awne.

After

After that whan Jeſus perceiued all
thinges were perfourmed : that the
ſcripture might be fulfilled: He ſayde,
I thriſt, There ſtode a veſſel ful of vi=
neger by: Thē thei filled a ſpōge with
vineger, ⁊ wound it about with yſope
and put it to hys mouthe. Aſſone as
Jeſus had receiued of the vineger, he
ſaid, it is finiſhed, ⁊ bowed his heade
⁊ gaue vp the goſt. The Jewes then
becauſe it was the Saboth euen, that
the bodies ſhould not remeyne vpon
the croſſe on ỹ Saboth day (for that
Saboth daye was an hyghe day) be=
ſought Pilat that theyr legges might
be brokē, and that thei might be takē
doune. Thē came the ſouldiours and
brak the legges of the fyrſt, and of the
other which was crucified with Jeſ⁹
But whan thei came to Jeſus, ⁊ ſaw
that he was dead alredye, thei brake
not his legges : but one of the ſouldi=
ours with a ſpeare, thruſt him into ỹ
ſyde, ⁊ furth with came there out blud
and water : ⁊ he that ſaw it bare re=

U.j.   cord

cord, & his record is true, & he knoweth that he saieth truth that ye might beleue also: for these thiges wer done that the scripture should be fulfylled: ye shal not breake a bone of him. And againe another scripture saith: Thei shall se him whom they haue persed.

After ý Ioseph of Aramathia (which was a disciple of Iesus: but secretlye for feare of the Iewes) besought Pilat that he might take doune the body of Iesus, And Pilat gaue him licēce. And ther came also Nicodemꝰ which at the begynnyng came to Iesus by night, and brought of mirrhe, & aloes mingled together about an hundreth pound weyght. Then tooke they the body of Iesu and wound it in linnen clothes wyth ý odours as the maner of the Iewes is to burye. And in the place wher Iesus was crucified, was a garden, and in the garden a new sepulchre, wherin was neuer mā layd. Ther layd they Iesus because of the Iewes Saboth euen, for the sepulchre was nygh at hand

Prayers of the

Passion of our sauiour Christ,
Blessed be the father, and the sonne, and the
holy ghoste.
Let vs praise him and exalt him, world without ende.

Lmighty god, our heuē
ly father, thy mercy ⁊
goodnes is ifinit ⁊ with
out mesure. It is thi mer
cye ⁊ no goodnes ꝑ was
in vs whiche moued the to sende into
the worlde thyne onely begotten eternal sonne to take our nature vpō him
and therinto worke the misteri of our
redēpcion and saluacion, according
as thou haddest appointed ⁊ haddest
spokē before by the mouthes of al thy
prophettes, which were from the beginning. Also it was thy blessed will
thy merci and goodnes towardes vs
that thy heauenly son did suffre per-
secution, trouble ⁊ aduersitie, betray-
ed of his awne frend and disciple Iu-
das, was trayterously takē aud caried

A.ij.   A=

away, to be falsly accused and vniustly condemned, to be cruelly bet & scourged. And fynally, wyth most scornful rebukes, to be put to most painful & shamful death that could be deuised. Al thys, O heauenly father, was done through thi mercy and blessed wil for our sakes, not only to answer & satisfy thi iust wrath and angre, which we had deserued bothe for the offences of our first parentes, & yet dayly doo deserue by transgressyng thy holy commaundementes: but also to restore vs agayn vnto thy grace and fauoure, to indue vs with thy heauenly gyftes, þ we myght serue the in holynes & righteousnes al the dayes of our life. And fynally to make vs by the fre benefite of thy derely beloued sonnes passion, & the pryce of hys most precious blud partners wyth hym of hys infynite & vnspeakeable glory & blysse in heauē Wherfore, O heauenly father we beseche þ powre vpon vs thyne holy spyryt & make vs in our heartes clearly to se

and

& moſt ſtedfaſtly to beleue this thyne
infinite gratious goodnes ſhewed &
geuen vnto vs by thyne awne ſonne
our ſauiour Jeſus Chꝛiſt, & with this
beleſe, make vs to put al our cōfidēce
& hope of ſaluation in hym, whō thou
haſt apoynted to be our only redemer
and ſauiour, Make vs alway to ren=
dꝛe vnto the moſt humble and hartie
thankes foꝛ thyne incompꝛehenſible
mercy and goodnes towarde vs. Fi=
nally, make vs to pꝛofeſſe the death of
thy dearly beloued ſonne in renoun=
ſyng and foꝛſakyng al ſynne, that we
may playnly appere to ryſe with him
in newnes of life, in righteouſnes, in=
nocency, and all true holynes, and af=
ter this lyfe to reigne wt him in euer=
laſtyng gloꝛy. Heare vs our heauenly
father, foꝛ our Loꝛde Jeſus Chꝛiſtes
ſake. Amen.

ALmighty God our heauenly ij.
father we beſech thi gratious
goodnes, that likewyſe as thi only be
gotten and derely beloued ſonne oure

sauiour Jesus Christ according to his
blessed wil, suffered willingly death &
bitter passion for our redemptiō and
salnatiō, hauyng therof forsight and
certain knowledge: So in like maner
whensoeuer it shalbe thy pleasure to
ley like crosse and affliction vpon our
backes, that we maye also wyllyngly
and patiētly beare it, to the true trial
of our fayth agaynst the latter daye, &
to thi euerlastyng glory. Hear vs our
heauenly father for our Lorde Jesus
Christes sake. Amen.

iij. **O**Ur sauioure and redemer Jesu
Christ, which in the last supper
with thine Apostles diddest cōsecrate
thy blessed bodye and blud vnder the
fourme of bread & wyne: Graunt vs
we besech the euer stedfastly to beleue
and kyndly to acknowledge thy infi=
nite and almyghtie power, thy incō=
prehensible loue toward vs, and that
we may alwaye worthely receiue the
same blessed sacrament accordyng to
thy holy ordinaunce: that thereby we
may

may obteyne increase of all godlynes
in vnitie of spirit, with the our hed, &
by the & thy spirit with al the company
of them that be truly thine, whiche be
thy spiritual and mistical body & our
spiritual & christen brethren: heare vs
our sauiour Christ for thi name sake.

ALmyghtie God our heauenly iiij
father which suffereddest Peter ý Apostle, presumyng of his awne
power myserably to fall, not onely in
the deniall of his master Christ for fear of an hādmayde, but also in forswe
ring, and cursyng of him selfe, if euer
he knewe him: Graunt vs we beseche
the mercifull father, that we neyther
presume of our awne might and power, but being in our awne hartes hum
bly & lowlye, knowledging our awne
infirmitie, frailtie and wekenes, may
euer in al our affayres, receyue at thy
myghtye hand, strength and comfort
to the acceptable perfourmāce of thi
holy & blessed wil. Hear vs our heauē
ly father, for our lord Jesus Christes
sake. Amen.

v. OUr blessed sauiour Jesu Christ,
or which in that great heuines of
thy soule, and intollerable angupshe,
which thou susteinedst before thi pas=
sion, diddest fall doune vpon thy face
in prayer vnto thy heauenlye father,
geue vs grace and the ayde of thy ho=
ly spirit, that we lykewise in al heui=
nes of mynd & troubles of this world
runne euermore by most humble and
instant praier vnto the aide and com=
fort of our heuély father. Here vs our
sauior Christ, for thy name sake. Am

vj. ALmightie God eternal father
we do remēbre, that in the cō=
demnation of thyne awne derely be=
loued sōne, that most innocent lambe
our sauiour Jesus Christ, the iudge
dyd sit, witnesses wer brought, Christ
was presented and cōdemned, and all
truth there was troden vnder fote, al
vnrighteousnes did reigne, and inno=
cency was condemned. O most grati=
ous lord and father, graunt vnto our
heades and rulers, that thei mai euer
in

in all theyr iudgementes iudge accor
dyng to true iustice and equitie with=
out corruption, partialite and wicked
dissimulation, to the oppressió of wic=
kednes , and to the maintenaunce of
thy euerlastyng truth, iustice, honor, &
glory. Heare vs our heauenly father,
for our lord Iesus Christes sake. Am.

A prayer in the mornyng.

O Lorde God almyghtie,
to whom & before whom
al thynges are manifest
and playne, which suffe=
rest not a Sparrowe to
light on the groúd with
out thy prouidence, & which in tymes
past by thy holy spirit dyddest guyde
our forefathers, Abraham, Isaac and
Iacob in thy pathes and wayes: and
agaynst the goyng of young Toby in
to a straunge countri, diddest prouide
thy holye angell and messenger to be
his guyde: Graunt me, this day , most
wretched synner (whom by thy word
thou doest encorage to call vpon thee

Aa.i. in

in all tymes of nedes and necessities)
that I may haue thy holy spirit to di=
rect my pathes and waies this daye,
that I may walke accordyng vnto thi
godly will and pleasure, profyt of my
neyghboure and glorye of thy name:
whiche lyuest & reignest world with=
out ende. Amen.

A prayer at your vprysyng

O Lorde Iesu Christ, whiche
art the very bryght sonne of
the world, euer risyng, neuer
fallyng, which with thy hol=
some looke engendrest, preseruest, no=
rishest, and makest ioyfull al thynges
that are in heauē and ye arth: Shyne
fauourably I beseche the vnto my spi=
rit, that the nighte of synnes and my=
stes of errours driuen awai by thy in=
ward lyght, I may walke all my lyfe
without stomblyng and offence, com=
ly as in the day tyme, beyng pure frō
the workes of darkenes. Graunt thys
o lord, whiche liuest & reignest with ye
father & ye holy gost for euermore. Amē

A prayer

A prayer before ye go to bed

O Lorde, whiche art onelye God
true, gracious & merciful, which
comaundest them that loue thy name
to caſt feare and care from them, and
to caſt it on the, promiſyng moſt mer=
cifully thy ſelfe to be their protectoure
from their enemies, theyr refuge in
daunger, theyr gouernor in the daye,
their light in darknes, & their watche=
man on the nyght alſo, ne uer to ſlepe,
but to watch continuallye for the pre-
ſeruyng of thy faithful: I beſeche thee
of thy bounteful goodnes (O lord) to
forgeue me where in I haue offended
the this day, and to receyue me vnder
thy protection this night, that I may
reſt in quietnes both of bodye & ſoule.
Graunt myne eyes ſlepe, but let myne
hert watch perpetually vnto the, that
the weken es of the fleſhe cauſe me not
to offend the lord. Let me at al tymes
fele thy goodnes towarde me, that I
be at al times ſtyrred to praiſe the, late
and early and at midde day thy praiſe

Aa.ij.   be

be in my mouth , and at midde nighte
Lord instruct me in thy iudgementes
that all the course of my life beyng led
in holines and puritie, J maye bee in=
duct at last into the euerlastyng rest,
which thou hast promised by thy mer=
cy to theim that obey thi word (o lord)
to whom be honour, prayse and glory
for euer. Amen.

A prayer for to trust in God

The begynnyng of the fal of mã
was trust in him selfe. The be=
gynnyng of the restoryng of man was
distrust in him selfe and trust in God.
O most gracious and most wise guid
our sauiour Christ, which doest leade
them the right way to immortal blesⸯ
sednes , which truly and vnfainedlye
trustyng in the, cõmit themselfe to the:
Graunt vs, that like as we be blynde
and feble in deede , so wee maye take
and repute our selfs, that we presume
not of oure selfes, to se our selfes , but
so far to se, that alway we maye haue
the before oure eyes to folowe the, be=
yng

yng our guid to be redy at thy cal most
obediently, and to commyt our selues
wholy vnto the, that thou whiche on=
ly knowest the wai, mayst lede vs the
same way vnto our heauēly desyres:
To the with the father and the holye
ghost be glory for euer. Amen.

A prayer for patience in trouble. Psal, lx

NOw hast thou O lord, humbled
& plucte me doune: I dare now
vnneth make my praiers vnto the, for
thou art angry with me, but not with
out my deseruyng. Certaynly I haue
synned Lorde, I confesse it, I will not
denie it. But oh my God, pardon my
trespasses, release my dettes, rendre
nowe thy grace agayne vnto me, stop
my woundes, for I am all to plaged
and beatē, yet lorde, this notwithstā=
dyng I abyde patiently, & gene myne
attendaunce on the, cōtinually way=
tyng for relefe at thy hande, and that
not without skyl: for I haue receiued
a token of thy fauour and grace tow=
ardes me, I meane thy worde of pro=

Aa. iij.   mes

mise concernyng Christe, who for me
was offered on the crosse for a raun-
some, a sacrifice, and price for my syn=
nes . wherefore accordyng to that thy
promise defend me lorde by thy ryght
hand, and geue a gracious eare to my
requestes, be thou my staye in perilles
for all mannes staies are but vayne.
Beate doune therfore myne enemies
thine awne self with thy power, whiche art my onely aider and protector,
O Lorde God almightie. Amen.

A prayer for concord of Chri=
stes churche, Psal, lxviii

ARise Lorde, let thine enemies
be scattered, thy haters put to
flyght, the righteous & Christes disciples make pleasaūt & mery: let theim
syng prayses and pleasaūt songes vn=
to thee, let them blow abrode thy ma-
gnificēce, let them most highly auaū-
ce thy maiestie, let thy glory grow, let
the kyngdome of Christ from heauen
emōg the chosen be enlarged: be thou
the father of the fatherlesse , the iudge
of

of the widowes , and the protector of
them, namely whom the world forsa=
keth, whose consciences bee troubled
whom the worlde pursueth for Chri=
stes sake. Whiche bee nedy & wrapped
full of misery. In thy house o lord, let
vs dwell in peace and concord, geue vs
al one hart, one mynd, one true inter-
pretacion vpon thy worde. Plucke of
the bandes aswel from the consciences
as from the bodies of the myserable
captiues and of them also which (as
yet bee hedged in within the listes of
death and vnaduisedly striue agaynst
grace . How drie (Lorde) is the flocke
of thyne heritage= I praie thee poure
doune largely the showers of thy grace, let a more plenteous fruitfulnesse
chaunce, let thy people be strengthned
with thy spirite. Graunt vs Lorde thy
worde abondantly, so that there maye
be many preachers of thy gospel which may within themselfes holily con-
spire and agre. Lette thy churche the
spouse of Christe deale large spoyles
                                    of

of the conquered Sathan. Al that beleue in thee , by Christ(o lorde God of
health)mought lift the vp with prai-
ses , mought renoume thee and extoll
thee . We be entred into the voyage of
saluacio. Conduct vs luckely vnto the
port , that beyng deliuered by thee fro
the very death we may escape ¢ come
to the very life. Finish the thyng thou
hast begon in vs, make vs encrease fro
faithe to faithe , leaue vs not to oure
awne wil and choyse, for it is slippery
and redy to fall. To the thuderboltes
of thy word put violece, that we maie
geue the glory to thee alonly. Geue to
thy people courage ¢ power to with-
stand synne, and to obey thy worde in
all thynges , o Lorde God moste glorious and excellent ouer all. Amen.

A prayer agaynst the enemies of Christes trouth. Psalme, cxxix,

DEliuer me o lord , fro the vngodly and stiffe necked persones , for
thou seest how in their hartes thei y-
magin mischef, ¢ haue greate pleasure

to

to picke querelles, their toungues bee more sharpe then any Adders styng. And vnder their lippes lurketh poyson of adders: but o mercifull lorde, let me not fall into their handes, that thei hãdle me not after their awne lustes. Thou onely arte my God, thou muste heare my piteous plaint, lord that rulest altogether, thou art the strengthe and power of my defence, be thou as a salet on my hed whensoeuer the vngodlye shall assaulte me, and suffre thou not the wicked thus to prosper in their matters. Suffre not their croked and malicious stomackes to increase, and spitefully reuile the. Loke vpon thy poore wretches cause, and ridd me out of these daily greuãces: thẽ shall I with a right vp hart and pleasaunt countenaunce extoll and magnifie thi holy name. Amen.

A prayer to kepe the toungue and to eschue
the infection of the world Psal cxl

TO the I cry o Lorde, heare me spedily, let my prayer bee as a

sweete

swet tast & sauor in thy presence, & the liftyng vp of myne handes as an euenyng sacrifice. Lorde set a watche aboute my mouth, kepe my lippes and my toungue also, that thei speake nothyng amisse (as do the vngodly) but thei cal purely and hartely vpon the, and report thy worthy prayses. Bow not my harte to lust after euill, nor to folowe the fashion of the wicked and abhominable sinners, least I happen to cloke my wickednes with other synnes as hipocrites do. Let me not liue as thei would haue me do, but rather as it shall best please thee. let me not approue neither their counsailes, nor their deedes, though thei cast neuer so Godly a shewe and faire face to the worlde. Let me not herken to the tisynges and swecte baites of the vngodly, whiche counsaill me to filthy & vncleane thynges : but rather let me g: ue good eare to the righteous and godly mã though he sharpely correct and chide me. Let me alwaye haue a

ready

redy iye towarde thee only, in thee to
trust & to apply my self vnto the. Cast
not awaye my soule, neither suffre it
not to perishe. Kepe me that I be not
tāgled with the snares of the vngod=
ly, and from the priuy trappes of ma=
licious persons saue me. Defende me
lorde through thy grace, for in all our
awne deuises & workes, can nothyng
be found sure for vs to trust vpon.

The prater of any captiue, accordyng to the
forme of Dauid when he was hid in
the caue. Psalme. C. xlii.

With my voice I cryed to the, a=
fore the I opē my lamentaciōs
in thy bosome I disclose the secrete
worde of myne hart, my dolors & gri=
fes I shewe vnto thee, mine hart is al
most lyke to brast, so greate is my dis=
comforture. Thou knowest al my fa=
shions, O lorde, and thou seest well e=
nough howe the vngodly haue layed
theirs snares for me. Loo, I cast mine
iye on thys side & that side, aswell on
my frendes as on my kynsfolkes, but

Bb.ij   all

all in vayne, none of them all helpeth
me. And againe, I cānot runne away
I am so laden and ouercharged with
irons. O lord mi maker & father now
vnto the I crye, thou arte myne onely
shote anker, defence & help. Thou art
my porcion and heritage in all coun=
treis, yea, I haue none other possessiō
but thee onely. To thee therefore I
sticke altogether, knowyng certainly
that nothyng can go amisse with me.
Cōsidre then my lamētable cōplainte
beholde, how I am lowe brought frō
the cruell persuers, whiche be muche
more of power then I am. Defend me
deliuer me from this prison & horrible
feare of syn and death, that I may set
out thy name. All the sainctes aswell
angels as men make sute for me, desi=
ryng the for my comforte. Thei shall
not cease vntill thei obtein their re=
quest. I meane vntil thou forgeue me
my synnes, & sende me comforte in this
distresse, with pacience and long suffe=
ryng. This once obteined, the godly
folke

folke shall flocke about me , & shal not
stint to geue thee thankes, when they
se that thou riddest me furthe of these
daungiers , to the highe prayse of thy
name. Lord be merciful vnto vs, take
part with vs, then shal we for euer lift
vp & magnify thy glorious name. Am̄

In great trouble of conscience Psal cxxxiii

LOrde heare my prayer, receiue my
supplicacion, herken to my plaint
for thy ryghteousnesse . Trye not the
law with thy seruaunt, for truly then
shal no liuyng mā be found vngiltie:
yea, not one of thy sainctes should escape quite at the barre , onlesse thou
graunt him thy gracious pardon. in-
somuche, euen the very starres be not
pure and faultles afore thee . In the
angels thou foūdest synne: now myne
enemies hūt for my soule, thei beate &
driue it doune, thei thrust it into darke
dungeons, where felons cōuict & con-
dēpned to death, wer wont to be kept
My spirite is sorowfull , my harte is
heauy & sad within my brest:to thee I

holde vp my handes, requiring the of
mercy. For lyke as the drye grounde
longeth for a showre of rayne, so my
soule thinketh long till it haue thyne
helpe and succoure, here me spedely: if
thou do not, I am in dispaire, my spirit is all wery of this bondage, I haue
bid my life farwell: wherfore O god,
hide not thy face that I be not like vn
to those, that be hurled into the pit of
dampnatio. After this night of myse-
ry ouerpassed, let the pleasaunt mornyng of comfort luckely shyne on me,
that by tyme I may here and feele thy
goodnes, for in the is all my trust: poit
me the way that I shall walke in, for
if thou be not my guide: I must nedes
wander and stray out of the way. To
the lord I lift vp my soule, & that with
al my hart, I besech the, take me furth
of myne enemies handes. Thou only
art my succour and sauegard. Teache
me to woorke whatsoeuer shalbe thy
pleasur for thou art my God. Let thy
good spirit conduct me into the lande
of

of the liuyng, encourage iny spiryt for
thi names sake: furth of al these trou=
bles, for thy righteosnes deliuer me.
Destroye myne enemies, as thou arte
gratious & fauozable towardes me.
Those that wil worke me sorowe and
grief plucke furth of the waye, for I
am thy seruaunt and for thy sake suf=
fre I all thys hurly burly. As thou
art God: so helpe thou me. Amen.

A prayer of the churche agaynste
synnes. Sapien. rb.

Thou (O our God) art swete long
suffering, and true, & with mercy
orderest thou all thynges for if we sin=
ne, yet are we thine, for we knowe thy
greatnes. If we sinne not then are we
sure that with the we bee alowed: for
to knowe the, is perfect righteousnes,
yea, and to knowe thy righteousnes
and power, is the rote of immortalitie

In warres the prayer of kyng Asa
ii. Paralipo. riiii

Lorde, it is all one with thee, to hel=
pe theym that haue nede, wyth
fewe oz with many: helpe vs O Lord
oure

our god, for we trust in the, and in thi
name be we come agaynst this multi=
tude. Thou art the lorde our God, let
no man preuayle agaynst the. Amen.

The prayer of Manasses kyng of
Juda. ii Paralipo xxxvi

O Lord almightie, God of oure fa=
thers Abraham, Isaac and Ja=
cob, and of the iust sede of them, whi=
che hast made heaue & earth, with all
the ornamentes therof, which hast or=
deined the sea by the word of thi com=
maunde ment, which hast shut vp the
depe, and hast sealed it for thy fearfull
and laudable name, drad of all men, &
honorable before the face of thy pow=
er. Thi fierce anger of thretnyng is a=
boue measure heuy to synners, but the
mercy of thy promise is great and vn=
serchable, for thou art the Lord God
most high aboue al the earth, long suf=
feryng, and excedynge mercifulll and
sory for the malice of men. J haue pro=
uoked thine anger, and haue done euil
before the, in commyttyng abominati=
ons

ons & multiplieng of offences . And
nowe, I bowe the knees of my harte,
requiring goodnes of the O lorde. I
haue synned lord, I haue synned, and
knowe my wickednes, I desire the by
praier, O lord forgeue me: O lord forgeue me, & destroy me not with myne
iniquities, neither do thou alwaye remember my euils to punish them, but
saue me (whiche am vnworthy) after
thy great mercy, and I wil praise the
euerlastyngly, al the daies of my lyfe:
for al the power of heaue praiseth the,
and vnto the belongeth glory, worlde
without ende. Amen.

The oration of Job in his moste greuous
aduersities and losse of goodes, Job i

NAked came I out of my mothers wombe, and naked shall
I returne again. The lord gaue, and
the lorde hath taken away , as it hath
pleased the lord so is it done: now blessed be the name of the lord. Amen.

A prayer of Hieremy, Hieremy. xvii

HEale me (O lord) and I shalbe
hole, saue thou me, and I shalbe
Cc.i.   saued

saued, for thou art my prayse . Bee not
thou terrible vnto me o lord, for thou
art he in whome I hope. when I am
in perill ,let my persecutours be con=
founded,but not me: Thou shalt bring
vpon them the time of their plage and
shalt destroy them right sone. Amen.

A prayer of Hieremy. Hieremy.xxxi.

O Lorde,thou hast chastne d me,
and thy chastenig haue I recei=
ued as an vntamed calf. Couert thou
me and I shalbe conuerted , for thou
art my lord god, for assone as thou di=
dest turne me I repēted my selfe: And
when I vnderstode, I smote vpō my
thigh, I confessed & was ashamed be=
cause I suffred ȳ reproch of my youth

A prayer of Salomon,for a competent
lyuyng.Prouer.xxx.

T wo thynges I require of thee,
that thou wilt not deny me be=
fore I dye . Remoue from me vanitie
and lies,geue me neither beggery nor
riches,only graunt me a necessary li=
uyng, least if I be to ful I might hap=
pelye be intised to denye the,and saye:

what

what felowe is the lorde: or constrayned throug pouertie, I might fal vnto stealyng, and to forswere the name of my God. Amen.

A prayer for obteinyng of wisedom. Sapi.ir

OD of our fathers, and lorde of mercy, thou that haste made all thinges with thy word, and ordeined man through thy wysedome, that he should haue dominion ouer the creatures whiche thou hast made, that he shuld order the world accordyng to equitie and righteousnes, and execute iudgement with a true hart, geue me wisedōe, which is euer aboute thy seat and put me not oute from emong thy children, for I thy seruaũt and sonne of thy handmayde, am a feble person of a short tyme, and to yong to the vnderstandyng of thy iudgement & lawes: yea, though a man be neuer so perfect emong the chyldren of men, yet if thi wisdome be not with him, he shail be nothyng worth: Oh send thy wysedome out of thy holy heauens, and frō

Cc.ij.   the

the throne of thi maiestie that she may
be with me,and labour with me,that
I may knowe what is acceptable in
thy sighte. For she knoweth and vn=
derstandeth all thynges,and she shal
conduct me ryght soverly in my wor=
kes,& preserue me in her power. So
shal my workes be acceptable.Amen
The prayer of Jesus the sonne of Syrach in
necessitie,& for wisedom Ecclesi.the last Chapi.

I Thanke the O lorde and kyng
and prayse the o God my sauior
I will yelde prayses vnto thy name.
Thou hast deliuered my bodye from
destruction,for thou arte my defender
and helper from the snare of the false
tong,and from them that are occupi=
ed in lyes. Thou hast bene my helper
from suche as rose against me,& hast
deliuered me accordyng to thy greate
mercy,& for thi holy names sake,thou
hast deliuered me from the roaring of
them that prepared them selues to de=
uoure me out of the handes of suche as
soughte after my life, from the multi=
tude

tude of them that trouble me & wente
about to set fire vpō me on euery syde
so that I was not brente in the middes of the fyre. From the depe of hell
thou deliueredst me, frō the vncleane
tōug, from lyyng wordes, frō the wicked iudge, and from the vnrighteous
tōug. My soule shal praise the lord vn
to death, for my life drewe nigh vnto
hel downeward. Thei compassed me
round aboute on euery side, and there
was no man to helpe me. I looked a-
boute me, if there were any man that
woulde sucour me, but ther was none
Then thought I vpon thy mercy O
lorde, & vpon thy actes that thou hast
done euer of old, namely, that thou de-
liuerest suche as put their trust in the
and riddest them out of the handes of
the false Paninis: thus lifted I vp my
prayer from the earth, and prayed for
deliueraunce from death. I called v-
pō the lord the father of my lord, that
he would not leaue me without helpe
in the day of my trouble, & in the time

of the proude: I wyll prayse thy name
continually, yeldyng honor and thankes vnto it and so my prayer is heard
Thou sauest me from destructio and
delyuerest me from the vnrighteous
time. Therefore will I knowledge,
and praise the, and auaunce the name
of the lorde. Whe I was yet but yong
or euer I went astray, I desired wysedome opely in my prayer, I came ther
fore before the temple and I sought it
very busely, and I wil seke for it to my
last houre. Then will it floryshe vnto
me as a grape that is soone ripe. My
hart reioysed in it, then went my fote
the ryghte waye: yea, from my youth
sought I after it, I bowed doue myne
eare a litle, and receiued it, I found in
my selfe muche wisedome & prospered
greatly in it. Therfore wil I geue the
glory vnto hym that geueth me wisedome, for I am aduised to do thercaf-
ter, I wil be gelous to ciene vnto that
is good, so shall I not bee confouded.
My soule hath wrestled with it, and I
haue

haue bene diligēt to be occupied in it
I lifted myne handes on highe, then
was my soule lightened through wisdome, so that I knowledge my folishnes, I oꝛdꝛed my soule after it I foūd her in clennes. I had my harte in it from the beginning, and therfoꝛe shal I not be foꝛsaken. My harte longeth after it, & therefoꝛe I gat a good treasure. Through it the loꝛd hath geuen me a new tōg, wherwith I wil pꝛaise him. Oh come vnto me ye vnlearned, & dwel in the house of discipline, withdꝛawe not your selues from it, but cōmon of these thinges, foꝛ your soules are very thirsty. I opened my mouth and spake. Oh come and by wysdome without mony, and bowe doune your necke vnder her yocke, & let your soule receiue discipline, it is euen at hand & redy to be found. Beholde with your eyes, how I haue had but litle laboꝛ & yet haue much rest. Oh receiue wisdome, and ye shal receiue plenty of siluer and golde in your possession. Let
your

your mynde reioyce in her mercy, and
be not ashamed of her praise, woorke
your woorke betimes, & she shall geue
you your reward in due tyme.

A prayer to speake the worde of God
boldely. Act. iiii.

LOrd, thou art god whiche hast
made heauen and earth, the sea
and all that in them is, whiche by the
mouth of thy seruaūt Dauid hast said
whi did the Heathē rage and the people imagyn vain thynges: The kynges of the earthe stode vp, and the rulers came together againste the lorde
and against his Christe. For surely a-
gaynst thy holye sonne Jesus whom
thou hast anoynted, both Herode and
also Poncius pilat with the Panims
& the people of Israel gathered them
selfs together to do euen whatsoeuer
thyne handes and thy counsail deter-
mined before to be done. And now
lorde beholde their thretenynges, and
graunt vnto thy seruauntes to speke
thy worde with al cōfidence, and that
thou

thou wilt stretch furth thyne hand, to
thintēt that healyng, signes and wō=
ders maye be done by the name of thy
holy sonne Jesus. Amen.

A prayer for the peace of the Churche.

LOrd Jesꝰ Christ which of thine
almightines madest al creatu=
res both visible and inuisible, whiche
of thy godly wisedome gouernest and
settest al thinges in most goodly ordre
which of thine vnspeakeable goodnes
kepest, defēdest, and furtherest al thin=
ges, which of thy depe mercy restorest
the decaied, renewest the fallē, raysest
the dead: Uouchesafe (we pray the) at
last to cast doune thy countenaunce v=
pon thy welbeloued spouse the church
but let it be that amiable & mercyfull
countenaunce wherwith thou pacifi=
est al thynges in heauen, in earth, and
whatsoeuer is aboue heauen and vn=
der the earth. Uouchsafe to cast vpon
vs those tendre and pitifull eyes with
which thou ones didest behold Peter
that great shepherde of thy churche, &

DD.j.   furth

furthwith he remembred hym selfe &
repented with whiche eies yͤ once dydest vewe the scatered multitude, & wert
moued with compassion, that for lack
of a good shepherd, thei wandered as
shepe dispersed and staied a sunder.
Thou seest (O good shepherde) what
sundry sortes of wolues haue broken
into thy shepecotes, of whome euery
one cryeth: here is Christ, here is christ
so that if it were possible the very perfect persons should be brought into er-
rour. Thou seest with what wyndes
wyth what waues, with what stormes thy sely shyppe is tossed: thy ship
wherein thy litle flocke is in perill to
be drouned. and what is nowe lefte,
but that it vtterly sincke and we al pe-
ryshe: Of this tempest and storme we
maye thanke our awne wickednesse &
sinfull liuyng, we espie it wel and confesse it, we espi thi righteousnes: & we
appele to thi mercy, which (according
to the Psalme of thy Prophet) sur-
mofited al thy workes, we haue now
suf-

ffered much punishment , beyng tou=
sed with so many warres , consumed
with suche losses of goodes, skourged
with so manye sortes of diseases and
pestilences, shaken with so mani flud=
des, feared with so mani straūge sigh=
tes from heauen, and yet appere ther
no wher any hauē or port vnto vs be=
yng thus tired and forlorne emonges
so straunge euyls, but stil euerye daye
more greuous punishmentes , & more
seme to hāg ouer our heades. we com=
playne not of thy sharpnes most tēdre
sauior, but we espye here also thi mer=
cy, forasmuch as much greuouser pla=
ges we haue deserued: but o most mer=
cyfull Iesu, wee beseche the that thou
wilt not considre ne weigh what is
due for oure deseruynges , but rather
what becommeth thy mercy, without
which nether the angels in heauē can
stād sure before the, much lesse we sell
vessels of clay. Haue mercy on vs, o re=
demer, which art easy to be ētreated,
not that we be worthy of mercye, but

Dd.ij.   geue

geue thou this glory vnto thine awne
name : suffre not that the Iewes, the
Turkes, and the rest of the Panimes
which either haue not knowne the, or
do enuy thi glory, shuld cōtinually tri=
ūph ouer vs, & say: where is their god
where is their redemer, where is their
sauior, where is their bridegrom, that
thei thus bost on: These opprobrious
wordes & vpbraidynges redoūd vnto
the o lorde whyle by our euylles, men
weigh and esteme thy goodnes: they
thynke we be forsaken whom thei see
not amended. Once when thou slepst
in the shippe, & a tempest sodenly ary=
syng, thretened death to all in the ship
thou awokest at the out crye of a few
disciples, & streight waye at thyne al=
mightie word the waues couched, the
wyndes fell, the storme was sodenlye
turned into a greatcalme. The dōbe
waters knewe their makers voyce.
Nowe in this farre greater tempest,
wherin not a fewe mens bodies be in
daunger, but mnumerable soules: we
beseche

besech the at the cry of thy holy church which is in daunger of drouning, that thou wilt awake. So many thousandes of menne do crye, Lorde, saue vs wee perysshe, the tempest is past mans power: yea, we se that the indeuours of them that would helpe it, do turne clene a contrary way. It is thy word that must do the dede lorde Jesu: Only say thou with a word of thy mouth Cease O tempest, and furthwith shal the desyred calme appere. Thou woldest haue spared so many thousandes of most wicked mē, if in the citie of Sodome had bene found but .x. good mē. Now here be so many thousandes of men which loue the glory of thi name which sigh for the bountie of thy house I wilt thou not at these mens prayers let go thine anger, and remember thine accustomed and olde mercyes: Shalt thou not with thy heuenly policye turne oure folye into thy glorie: Shalt thou not turn the wicked mēs euils to thy Churches good: For thy

mercy

mercy is wont then moste of al to suc=
cor, whē the thyng is with vs past re=
medy, and neither the might, nor wis=
dom of men can helpe it. Thou alone
bryngest thynges that be neuer so out
of ordre, into ordre agayn: which arte
the onelye aucthor and mainteiner of
peace. Thou framedst that old confu=
sion which we cal Chaos, wherin with
out ordre, without fashion confusely
lay, the discordāt seedes of thyngē, ɛ
wyth wonderfull ordre, the thynges,
that of nature fought together, thou
didest alie ɛ knit in a perpetuall band.
But how muche greater confusion is
this where is no charitie, no fidelitie,
no bōdes of loue, no reuerēce neither
of lawes nor yet of rulers, no agremēt
of opinions, but as it were in amisor=
dered quier euery man syngeth a con=
trary note. Emong the heauenly pla=
nettes is no discēsiō, all. iiij. elemētes
kepe their place, euery one do their of=
fice wherunto thei be appointed. And
wilt thou suffre thy spouse, for whose
sake

sake all thynges were made , thus by
continuall discordes to perishe & go to
wrecke. Shalt thou suffre the wicked
spirites , which be aucthors and wor=
kers of discord to beare such a swynge
in thy kingdō vnchecked? Shalt thou
suffre that strong capitayn of mischief
whom thou once ouerthrewest, again
to inuade thy tentes and to spoile thy
souldiers? when thou wert a mā here
conuersaunt emonges mē,at thy voice
fled the deuils. Send furth we beseche
thee o lord thy spirit which may drine
away out of the brestes of all thē that
professe thi name the wicked spirites,
masters of riote , of couetise, of vaine=
glory ,of carnall luste,of mischief, & of
discord. Creat in vs,o our god & king
a cleane hart, & renue thy holy spirite
in our breastes,plucke not frō vs thy
holy ghost. Rendre vnto vs the ioy of
thy sauyng health,and with thy prin=
cipall spirite , strengthen thy spouse &
the herdemeu thereof. By this spirite
thou reconciledst the yearthly to the
heauenly

heuēly, by this thou didest frame ¢ re-
duce so many tonges, ¢ so many nacions, so many sondꝛy soꝛtes of mē, into
one body of a churche, whiche body by
thesame spirit is knit to thee their hed
This spirit if thou wilt vouchsafe to
renue in al mens hartes, then shall also these foꝛein miseries cease, oꝛ if they
cease not, at lest thei shall turne to the
pꝛofit ¢ auaile of thē which loue thee.
Stey this confusion, set in oꝛdꝛe this
hoꝛrible Chaos (o loꝛd Iesu) let thy spirit stretch out it self vpō these waters
of euill waueryng opinions. And because thy spirit, whiche accoꝛding to
the pꝛophetes saiyng conceiueth all
thinges hath also the sciēce of speking,
make that like as vnto al them which
be of thy house, is al one light, one bap-
time, one God, one hope, one spirite: so
thei may haue also one voice, one note
¢ sōg, pꝛofessing one catholique truth.
when thou didst mount vp to heauen
triumphantly, thou threwest aboute
frō aboue thy pꝛecious thynges, thou
gauest

gauest gyftes among men, thou deltest
sundry rewardes of thy spirite. Renue
again from aboue thy old bositifulnes,
geue that thyng to thy churche nowe
faintyng & growing donneward, that
thou gauest vnto her shoting vp at the
first beginning. Geue vnto princes &
rulers the grace to stand in awe of the
that they so may guyde the common
weale as they should shortely rendre
accomptes vnto the, that art Kyng of
kynges. Geue wisdome to be alwaies
assistent vnto them, that whatsoeuer
is best to be doen, they maye espie it in
their myndes, and pursue the same in
their doinges. Geue to thy bishops the
gift of prophesy, that they may declare
& interprete holy scripture, not of their
awne brayne, but of thyne inspiring.
Geue them the threfold charitie which
thou once demaundest of Peter what
tyme thou didest betake vnto hym the
charge of thy shepe. Geue to thy prie=
stes the loue of sobernesse, & of chasti=
tie. Geue to thy people a good wyil too

folow thy cōmaundementes and a re-
dines to obey suche persones, as thou
hast appoincted ouer theim. So shal it
come to passe, if through thy gyfte thy
prīnces shal commaunde that thou re-
quirest, if thy pastors & herdmen shall
teache thesame, & thy people obey them
bothe, that the old dignitie and tran-
quilitie of the churche shall returne a-
gain with a goodly ordre vnto the glorye of thy name. Thou sparedst the
Niniuites appoincted to be destroyed
assone as thei conuerted to repentāuce
And wilt thou despyse thy house fallyng doune at thy fete, which in steade
of sacke cloth hath sighes, & in steade
of ashes teares: Thou promisedest for
geuenes to suche as turne vnto thee,
but this self thing is thy gift, a man to
turne with his whole hart vnto thee,
to thintent all our goodnes should re-
dounde vnto thy glory. Thou art the
maker, repaire thy woorke, that thou
hast fashioned. Thou art the releuer
saue that thou hast bought. T riset

the sauiour, suffre not theim to perishe
that doo hang on thee. Thou art the
lorde and awner, chalenge thy possession. Thou art the hed, helpe thy mem
bers. Thou arte the Kyng, geue vs a
reuerence of thy lawes. Thou art the
Prince of peace, breathe vpon vs bro-
therly loue. Thou art the God, haue
pitie on thy huble besechers: bee thou
accoding to Paules saiyng, all thynges in all men to thintent the whole
quier of thy church with agreing mindes & consonaunt voices for mercy obteined at thy handes, may geue thankes to the father, sonne, & holy ghost,
which after the moste perfect example
of concord bee destincted in propertie
of persones, & one in nature, to whom
be praise and glory eternally. Amen.

A praier for the keping of a good name.

That wiseman whiche was priuy
of thy secretes (o heauenly father)
taught vs that an honest name is a
treasure right precious, when he sayth:
better is it to haue a good name then

precious oyntmentes. But this so ex=
cellent and good thyng we neither can
get nor kepe, but by thi name and help.
How surely the well and founteine of
a good name is a fautclesse life. This
therfore in especial we demaunde and
craue of thee, O Lorde almightie, yet
neuerthelesse, forasmuche as oftenty=
nies innocencie and fauktlesse lyuyng
is not enough), neither yet a sure buck=
ler and defence, namely against suche
as vnder their lippes beare the poyson
of serpentes: yea, and oftentimes it hap=
peneth, that when we suppose to be a=
monges our trustie frendes, we dwell
with Ezechiell among scorpions and
venemous serpentes, we crie with thy
holy Prophetes, O Lorde, deliuer my
soule from wicked lyppes, & a gylefull
tonge, but if neuertheles it bee sene to
thy goodnes to exercise thi seruauntes
also with this affliccion, to the intent
they may better be brought to godly=
nes and perfeccion: Graunt (we praie
thee) that with Paule thy moste vali=

aunt

aunt champion we may by reproche
and glory, by infamy and good name
abide still in thy commaundementes,
trough Jesu Christ, which also hym
selfe (when he walked here in yearth)
was reuiled, slaundered, euil spoken of
and called to his tethe a Samaritan.
a wyne drynker, a deceiuer of the people, & one that had a deuill. Thesame
now reigneth with thee in glory together, with the holy ghost. Amen.

℃ A prayer against wordly carefulnes.

MOste dere and tender father, our
defender and norisher, indue vs
with thy grace that we maie cast of ye
great blyndnes of our myndes & carefulnes of wordly thynges, and maye
put our whole study & care in kepyng
of thy holy lawe. And that wee may
labor and trauaill for oure necessities
in this lyfe, like the birdes of the aire, &
the lilies of the field without care. For
thou haste promised to bee carefull for
vs, and haste commaunded that vpon
the we should cast all our care, wuiche

Ee. iii.

lyuest and reignest worlde without
ende. Amen.

A prayer against pride and vnchastnes.

OLhou Lorde father and God of
my life, let me not vse proudly to
loke, but turne away frō me all fylthy
desires . Take from me the lustes of
the body, let not the desires of vnclen-
nes take holde vpon me , and geue me
not ouer into an vnshamefast and ob-
stinat mynde. Amen.

Another prayer against pride.

OLord Christ in most mighty power, most meke, and in greatest
excellencie, moste lowlye: yea, of thyne
awne wil most humble, geue vnto me
thy mynd and spirite that I may knowledge my wekenes leuened & infec-
ted with malicioulnes, that through
thine example I may be humble and
meke, wh ch haue no cause to bost my
selfe . Thinges of the worlde be vncer-
tein, left to a short vse. The body is fa-
dyng, frayle and fylthy, the mynde is
blynde and frowarde, whatsoeuer I
haue

haue of myne awne, it is naught: if J
haue any goodnes it is of God, ɇ not
of me. Knowyng this feblenes of my
selfe, why should J magnyfie my selfe:
And specially sith thou lord of heauen
and yearth, being of suche wonderfull
excellency, diddest humble thy selfe to
the lowest state of men, graūt me true
humilitie, that J may be exalted to the
euerlastyng glory: which lyuest ɇ reignest with the father and the holy ghost
for euer. Amen.

℟ A prayer agaist enuie.

LOrd, the inuentour and maker
of all thynges, and the disposer
of thy giftes, which thou bestowest of
thy bounteous lyberalitie, geuyng to
each man more then he deserueth, vnto each mā sufficiētly, so that we haue
no cause of grudge or enuye, sith thou
geuest vnto al men of thine awne, and
vnto such as deserue it not, ɇ to eache
man sufficiently toward the heauenly
blessednes: graunt vs that we be not
enuious but quietly cōtent with the

iudgement, and the disposyng of thy
gyftes and benefites. Graunt vs to be
thankful for that we receiue, and not
to murmur secretly with our selues a=
gainst thy iudgement and blessed wyll
in bestowing thy fre benefites, but ra=
ther that we loue and praise thy boun=
teous liberalitie aswel in others as in
our selfe, and alwaies magnifie the o
lord, the well of al giftes and goodnes.
To the be glory for euer. Amen.

CA prayer against anger.

LOrde Iesu Christ whiche saidest,
whosoeuer is angry with his bro=
ther, shalbe giltie to iudgemēt: which
also doest reserue from time to tyme al
vengeaunce and displeasure to thy se=
crete and iust iudgemēt: Graunt vs of
thy great mercy, that by no maner of
occasion we fal not into disordering of
our selfe by anger and desyre of reuen=
ging, but that we may alway remem=
bre, not onely thy godly commaunde=
ment, which chargeth vs to do well to
them that hate vs, and to pray for thē

that

that say euyll by vs: but also that we bear in mind thi holy example, which didest pray for theym that cruelly crucified the. To the with the father and holy ghost be glory euerlastyng. Am.

A prayer in aduersitie.

O Lord God, without whose wil and pleasure a Sparrow dothe not fal vpõ the ground, seyng it is thi wil and permissiõ, that I shoulo be in this misery and aduersitie: Seing also that thou doest punish me with aduersitie, not to destroy me and cast me away, but to call me to repentaunce, & to saue me. For whõ thou louest, hym dost thou chastise: Furthermore seing affliction and aduersitie worketh pacience, and whoso pacientlye beareth tribulation, is made like vnto our sauiour Christ our hed: Finally, seyng that in al tribulation and aduersitie, I am in assuraunce of comfore at thy gratious hande. For thou hast commaūded me to cal vpõ the in the tyme of tribulation, and hast promysed to

hearc

heare and succour me: Grant me therfore, O almightie God, & merciful father, in al trouble and aduersitie to be quiet, without impacience & murmuryng, wythout discouraging & desperation, to prayse and magnifie the, to put my whole trust and confidence in the, for thou neuer forsakest thē that trust in the, but workest al for the best to them that loue the, and seke ỹ glory of thy holy name. To the be glorye for euer. Amen.

A prayer in prosperite.

I Geue the thākes o god almightie, which not al only hast indued me with thi giftes of nature, as reson, power & strēght, but also hast plētifully geuen me the substāuce of this world: I knowlege(o lord)that these thy giftes, and cōfesse with holy saint James that there is no perfecte nor good gyft but it commeth from the(o father of lightes)whiche geuest frely & castest no man in the teeth. I knowledge with the Prophete Agge, that
gold

gold is thine and siluer is thyne, and
to whom it pleseth the, thou geuest it,
to the godly that they may be thy dis=
posers and distributours thereof, and
to the vngodly to heape vp their dam
nation with all. wherefore my most
mercifull god, I humbly beseche and
desire of the to frame in me with thy
holy spirit a faythfil heart and redye
hand to distribute these thy good gyf=
tes accordyng to thy wil and pleasure
that I treasure not vp here wher the=
ues maye robbe, and mothes corrupt
but to treasure in thy heauely kyngdō
Wher nether these mai steale, nor moth
defile, to myne awne cōfort (whom of
thi mercy þ hast promised, to reward
therfore) to the good example of þ hū=
ble & weake of thy cōgregatiō, and to
the glory of thy name. To whō wyth
thy sōne & holy ghost be all honor and
prayse, world without ende. Amen.

A fruitfull prayer to be sayd at all tymes

O Merciful God, graunt me to co-
uet with a feruent mynde those

Ff.ij.   thyn=

thinges which may pleſe the, to ſerch
them wyſely, to knowe them truelye,
and to fulfyll theym perfectlye to the
laude and glorye of thy name. Order
my liuyng, ſo that I may do y̆ which
thou requireſt of me, & geue me grace
that I may optai thoſe thiges, which
be moſt conuenient for my ſoule. Good
Lord make my way ſure and ſtreight
to the, ſo that I fal not betwene proſ-
peritie and aduerſitie, but that in pro-
ſperous thinges I may geue the thã-
kes, & in aduerſitie be patient, ſo that
I be not lifte vp with the one, nor op-
preſſed with y̆ other. And that I may
reioyce in nothyng, but y̆ whiche mo-
ueth me to y̆, nor to be ſory for nothing
but thoſe thinges which draweth me
from the, deſiryng to pleaſe no bodye
nor fearig to diſpleaſe any beſides the
Lord let al worldly thiges be vyle vn
to me for the, let me not be mery with
the ioye that is without the, & let me
deſyre nothyng beſydes the. Let that
labour delight me whiche is for the, &
let

let al the rest weri me, which is not in the. Make me to lift vp my hart oft times to the, and whē I fal make me to thinke on the, and be sory with a stedfast purpose of amendement. My god make me humble wythout fainyng, mery without lightnes, sad without mystrust, sobre withoute dulnes, true without doublenes, fearyng the without desperation, trusting in the without presumption, tellyng my neighbours faultes without dissimulation teachyng them with wordes and examples without mockynges, obediēt withoute arguyng, patient withoute grudgyng, and pure without corruption. My most louyng lorde and God geue me a wakyng heart that no curious thought withdrawe me from the let it be so strong that no vnworthye affection drawe me backward, so stable, that no tribulation breake it. My lord. graunt me wit to knowe the, diligēce to seke the, cōuersatiō to please the ⁊, finallye, hope to embrace thee:

FF.iij.　　　　　　　fo

for þ precious bloud sake of that immaculate lambe our only sauiour Jesu Christ: To whom with the father & the holy ghost, thre persons and one God, be all honoure and glory world without ende. Amen.

Adeuout prayer vnto Jesu Christ called O bone Jesu

O Bounteful Jesu O swete Jesu O Jesu the sone of the pure virgin Mari, full of mercy and truthe, O swete Jesu after thi great merci haue pitie vpõ me. O benigne Jesu I pray the by the same precious bloude, that for vs myserable sinners thou werte content to shed inthe aulter of ý crosse that thou vouchsafe cleane to auoyde all wickednes, and not to despise me, humbly this requiryng, and vpõ thy most holy name Jesus callyng. Thys name Jesus is a swete name. Thys name Jesus is the name of helth. For what is Jesus but a sauiour: O good Jesus that hast created me, and with thy precious bloud redemed me, suffre me me not to be damned, whō thou haste made of nought. O good Jesꝰ let not my wickednes destroy me, whom thy almighty goodnes made and formed O good Jesu reknowledge ẏ is thine in me, and wipe cleane away that draweth me from the. O good Jesu whā time of mercy is, haue mercy vpon me neither confound me in the tyme of thy terrible iudgement. O good Jesu if I wretched sinner for my most greuous offences haue by thi very iustice deserued eternall payne, yet I appele from thy righteousnes, and stedfastly trust in thyne ineffable mercy. I dout not but thou wylte haue mercy vpon me like a mylde father and mercifull Lord. O good Jesu what profyt is in my bloud, sins that I must descend in to corruption. Certaynly they that be dead shall not magnifie the, nor lykewyse all they that go to hel. O moste merciful Jesu haue merci vpō me. O most swete Jesu deliuer me. O most meke Jesu be vnto me cōfortable. O

Jesu

Jesu accept me a wretched sinner ito the nūber of thē that shalbe saued. O Jesu the helth of them that beleue in the, haue mercy vpon me. O swete Jesu þ forgeuenes of al mi sines. O Jesu the sōne of the pure virgi Mari indue me with thy grace, wysdome, charitie, chastite and humilitie: yea, & sted fast patience in all my aduersities, so that I may perfitely loue the, and in the be glorified and haue my only delight in the, world without. ende. Amē

A prayer to be sayd at the houre of death.

OLord Jesu, which art the onlye health of al mē liuing and the euerlastyng lyfe of them whych dye in thy faith. I wretched sinner geue and submyt my selfe whole vnto thy most blessed wyll: And I beyng sure that the thyng cannot perysshe, whiche is committedvnto thi mercy : wyllingly nowe I leaue this frayle and wicked flesshe in hope of the resurrectiō which in better wise shal restore it to me agai I beseche the most merciful lord Jesu
Chryst

Christ, ҧ thou wylt by thy grace make strong my soule agaynst all temptacions, and that thou wilt couer and defend me with the buckeler of thy mercy against al the assaultes of the deuil. I see and knowledge that there is in my selfe no healpe of saluation, but all my confidence, hope and trust is in thy moste mercyfull goodnes. I haue no merites nor good woorkes whiche I may alledge before the: Of sinnes and euil workes (alas) I se a great heape, but through thy mercy I trust to be in the number of theim, to whome thou wilt not impute their synnes, but take and accept me for righteous and iust, and to be the inheritour of euerlasting lyfe. Thou mercifull lord werte borne for my sake: Thou dydest suffre bothe hunger and thirst for my sake, thou didest preache & teache, thou didest pray and fast for my sake: thou dydoest all good woorkes and dedes for my sake. Thou suferedst most greuous peines and tormentes for my sake. And finally, thou gauest thy moste precious body to die, and thy bloude to be shed on the crosse for my sake. Now most merciful sauiour, let al these thynges profit me, which thou frely hast geuen me that hast geuen thy selfe for me, let thy bloud clense and wash away the spottes and foulnes of my synnes. Let thy righteousnes hyde and couer my vnrighteousnes. Let the merites of thy passion and bloud be the satisfaction for my synnes. Geue me lord thy grace that my faith & saluacion in thy bloud wauer not in me, but euer be firme and constant, that the hope of thy mercy and life euerlastyng neuer decay in me that charitie waxe not colde in me: fynally, that the wekenes of my flesh be not ouercome with the feare of death: Graūt me merciful sauiour, that whē death hath shut vp the iyes of my body, yet that the iyes of my soule maie styll behold & loke vpō the, that when death hath taken away the vse of my tong and speche, yet that my hart may crie

crie and say vnto the: In manus tuas domini. commendo fpiritum meum, **that is to saye:** O lorde, into thy handes I geue and commit my soule. Domine Iefu accipe fpiritum meum: Lord Iefu, receiue my soule vnto the. Amen.

A generall confeffion of finnes vnto God.

O Moſt mercifull Lorde God and moſt tendre & dere father, vouchſafe I hartely beſeche the, to loke doune with thy fatherly iyen of pitie vpon me moſt vile & wretched finner, which lie here proſtrate in hart before the fete of thy botomeles mercy, for I haue finned againſt the throne of thy glory, and before the O father: infomuche that I am no more worthy to bee called thi fonne. Neuertheles, forafmuch as thou art the God and father of all comfort, & again deſireſt not the death of the finner, but lyke a true Samaritan takeſt thought of my fely wounded foule: Make me (I pray the) by infoundyng thy precious oyle of comfort into my woundes, ioyfully to runne

with the lost sonne into the lap of thyne
euerlastyng pitie. For lo, thou art my
hope and trust, in whom I only repose
my selfe, hauing in the full confidence
and faith, and so I say with very fayth
full hart, trusting in thy mercy, I beleue in the O God the father, in the O
God the sonne, & in the O God the holy ghost. iij. persones and one true and
also very God, beside whom I knowledge none other God in heauē aboue,
nor in ye earth beneth: yea, and I poore
sinner do accuse my selfe vnto the dere
father, that I haue sore and greuously
offended thy almightie goodnes and
maiestie in the committing of mine a-
boundaunt greuous and manifold sin
nes and wretchednes, for I haue not
kept the lest of thy most godly & blessed
commaundementes lyke as thy ryghteousnes may require and demaunde
the same of me. I haue (Isaic) not honoured the lyke my God, nor dread the
lyke my lord, loued the lyke my father
trusted in the lyke my creatour and sauiour.

niour. Thy holy and dredfull name
vnto whom all glory and honour be=
longeth, haue I vsed in vayne. I haue
not sanctified ý holy daies with wor=
kes which be acceptable vnto the, nor
instructed my neighbour in vertue ac=
cordyngly. I haue not honoured my
parentes nor bene obedient vnto them
through whom (as by an instrument)
thou hast wrought my commyng into
this world. The high powers and ru=
lers which take their authoritie of the
I haue not bene wyllyngly obedyent
vnto. I haue not kept mine hart pure
and clene from māslaughter: yea, had
not thy grace and mercy defended me
the better, I should haue commytted
the deede also. I likewise am not pure
from theft, nor from aduoutry, nor frō
false witnes bering, but haue in myne
hart and mynde wyshed and desyred
my neighbours goodes and thynges.
I haue folowed the greate prynce of
this world Satan (whiche hath bene
a lier euen from the beginning) in con=

cupiscence of the fleshe, in pride of ly=
uyng, in lyyng, in deceitfulnes, in leche
ry, in hatred and also enuy, in backby=
tyng, in dispaire, and also misbeleue.
My fyue wyttes haue I foulye misu=
sed and spente, in heryng, seyng, smel=
lyng, tastyng, and also felyng, whiche
thou hast geuen me to vse vnto thy ho=
nour and glorie, and also to the edifi=
cacion and profite of my neighboure.
But in what maner soeuer that I ha=
ue offeded and sinned against thy eter=
nall maiestie (for no mã knoweth tho=
roughly his synnes as thy Prophet
witnesseth) whether it hath bene by
daye or els by nyghte: yea, euen from
my chyldhod vnto this day, were it in
wordes, workes or thoughtes secretly
or openly: O my mercifull God I am
sory for it, euen from the very bottom
of my hart: yea, & my soule mourneth
for sorowe moste merciful father, that
I am not a thousand times sorier then
I am. Howe be it, in token of great re=
pentaũce (though all hartes be knowẽ
well

well ynough vnto the) J do knocke &
ftrike my breaft and faye in bitternes
of hart and foule: lord God and father
haue mercy, lord God fonne haue mercy, lorde God holy ghoft haue mercy.
Spare me of thy infinitie mercy dere
lorde nowe, and al the daies of my life
and let me haue parte of thine abun-
daunt grace, fo as J may chaunge my
finfull lyfe, and put out of me the olde
man with all his euill concupifcence,
and alfo ŷ J may dye vnto the worlde
and that the worlde, may bee vnto me
a croffe, and fo go furth in a newe life.
Strengthen me O lord in a true humble hart, in perfect loue hope and truft
in ŷ. Geue my foule the grace to defyre
the onely, in the only to reioyce and re-
pofe my felfe, and that J may vtterly
renounce and forfake the vayne affiaunce of this world, fo that thou may-
eft fynd me redy with the good ferua-
unt in ŷ midnight of my death, whiche
fhall fodenly ftele vpon me like a thefe
ere J bee ware. Bee thou vnto me at
that

that tyme of nede (O lorde) a towre of
strength, a place of refuge, and a defen=
sible God, namely agaynst the face of
the fende, who like a roryng Liō shal
be then moste redy to deuour, and aga=
inst desperaciō, which then shalbe bu=
sy to greue me. Let then thy comforte
cleue fast vnto me, thy mercy kepe me
and thy grace guyde me. Fetche then
again, lord God the father, that whi h
thy puisaunt might hath shapē:fetche
then again lord the sonne that which
thou hast so wisely gouerned & bought
with thy precious bloud. Take again
then lord holy ghost, that which thou
hast kept and preserued so louingly in
this region of sinne and vale of myse=
ry thre persones & one very God, vnto
whom be praise and honoure for euer
and euer. Amen.

¶ A praier against the deuill.

IEsu Christ our lorde, whiche by
the mouthe of the holy Apostle
saynct Peter, moste truely diddest saie
that our aduersary the deuill goeth a.
bout

bout like a roaring Lyon, seking whõ
he may deuour: he is busy and fierce,
and breketh in vpon vs, so that if thou
helpe not, he wil sone deceiue vs, with
his craft ouerturne vs, with his my=
ght and with his cruelnes teare vs in
peces. But if thou which hast vanqui=
shed him, wilt appere, but as it were
afarre of, thou wilt make hym afrayd
and wyth thy onely loke put hym to
flyghte. Vouchsafe O lorde to receyue
vs into thy garde, being but infantes
weke, feble & vnskylfull, least ẙ fierce
& cruel beast all to teare vs. We beare
before vs and shewe furth in this our
fyght the crosse thy banner, the crosse
thy triumph and victory, that our ene=
my may well knowe that we do oure
busines by thy counsayle, ayde, and
strength: to the be glory for euer. Amẽ

℣ For the desyre of the lyfe to come.

This my body is the very darke
& filthy prison of the soule, this
worlde is an exile, and a banishment:
this life is care and misery, but where

thou art O lorde there is the very coun-
try of libertie, and euerlasting blessednes. Stirre our mindes now and then
to remember so great felicitie: Poure
into oure hartes a desire of suche precious thinges, and of all thynges most
to be desired. Geue quietnes vnto our
minde, and graunt that we may haue
some taste of the euerlasting ioyes,
whereby these thinges of the worlde
may seme filthy, and be so lothful vnto
vs, whiche we seke for so ernestly, and
embrace so gredely, and reteine so surely, that we may refuse and dis-
pise these bitter and filthy
thinges, and moste fer-
uently desire the swet-
nes of thy familia-
ritie, in the whi-
che all good-
nes is con-
teyned.
To the be glo-
rye for euer. AMEN.

⸪

The ende of the Prymer.

¶ Imprinted at London,
the laſt date of Nouember, in the firſt yere
of the reigne of our ſouereigne
lord kyng Edvvard the. VI.
By Rychard Grafton.
printer to his moſte
royall Ma=
ieſtie.
In the yere of our L

M.D.XLVII.

Cum priuilegio adimpri=
mendum ſoium.

(1547)

CPSIA information can be obtained at www.ICGtesting.com
Printed in the USA
LVOW052334040312

271565LV00003B/167/P

9 781240 160051